DRAGGED INTO THE LIGHT

Truthers, Reptilians, Super Soldiers, and
Death Inside an Online Cult

Tony Russo

SECANT PUBLISHING
Salisbury, Maryland

Secant Publishing, LLC
P.O. Box 4059
Salisbury, MD 21803
www.secantpublishing.com

The names of principal characters in this book are those identified in court and police records. The names of some cult members may be aliases or online personae.

ISBN: 978-1-944962-93-7 (hardcover)
ISBN: 978-1-944962-94-4 (paperback)
ISBN: 978-1-944962-95-1 (ebook)

Library of Congress Control Number: 2021907488

Book cover design by ebooklaunch.com

For my wife, Kelly

CONTENTS

INTRODUCTION

"And if any one tried to loose another and
lead him up to the light,
let them only catch the offender, and they
would put him to death."

Plato, *The Republic*

I want to implicate you in this story the same way I was implicated. I want that realization to come to you the same way it came to me. I wasn't drawn to this story; it was suggested by a colleague. I'd just come off more than two years interviewing combat veterans for the *This Is War* podcast and was looking for something else to write about.

"Have you seen this Sherry Shriner reptile thing?" the colleague asked.

I saw Sherry's story as an introduction to a larger story about for-profit cults and internet scammers. When I dove deeper, though, her story's implications broadened as QAnon and other conspiracy actors and theories bubbled up into the mainstream.

Anthony Warner, the 2020 Nashville Christmas bomber, who espoused many of the beliefs I'm about to discuss, was reported to have written, "They put a switch into the human brain so they could walk among us and appear human." It's a description of the reptilian conspiracy espoused by the people I've dubbed the Shrinerites, nearly down to the word.

I watched a conspiracy theory-driven mob take over the US Capitol, I imagine, the way a true prophet might see their vague notions solidify, shadows of inklings emerging from the gray. Worse, I saw, and still see, the ripples. The obvious responses and reactions. Finger-pointing and think-piecing about how the internet breeds these beasts.

I'm here to tell you that the internet doesn't breed monsters any more than a coop breeds pigeons. We breed the monsters; the internet just lets them thrive. And as we wring our hands about what the internet does as if it has volition, we avoid responsibility. We avoid the truth. In this case, that conspiracy theory culture is a symptom of our crumbling belief in religion's ability to salve, and the farce of professional political discourse.

In many cases, the people who are most susceptible to these conspiracies and cults are those who believe most in God and country and are heartbroken by their betrayal. It's not just that religious and political figures dodge leadership responsibilities. It's that their lies have cast the idea of safety, or even of stasis, into serious doubt.

Conspiracy theories replace their perceived chaos with order, their dissembling with fixed truths, and give lie to their claims of higher service. That's the appeal. To dismiss large communities of people as unwilling slaves to the corporate internet misses their search for certainty while relieving our complicity. Accepting their striving to understand as genuine, rather than as a result of some deeper madness, helped me understand the people in this story better.

The short answer to why they cling to their beliefs is the same as the reason you cling to yours: it is comfortable and safe. How and why they choose their beliefs is where we feel like we can step back and judge.

That was the hardest realization for me in reporting this book, and at times I fail to suspend judgment. It is so difficult not to be dismissive once we realize that, in the conspiracy theorist's reality, incompatible or inconsistent claims live together happily. Orgone, a mystical substance invented from whole cloth by a respected psychologist, stands out as the most impenetrable idea in this story. It works under such conditional rules as to be baffling in its meaninglessness. Yet people's lives have been changed and ruined by it.

Another difficulty was the temptation to understand and refute the conspiracy theories or to dismiss them out of hand. I tried to find middle ground where I understood well enough to explain without getting caught up in what I knew was utter nonsense. For example, I struggled to navigate the murky rules for how and when reptilians take over a person's body, but since that doesn't ever happen, I leave the nebulous reasoning untouched.

The conspiracies for me are a distraction from what's going on, which is a predictable amount of religious charlatanism feeding on soul-crushing fear and loneliness.

What I've come to discover is that beneath the accounts of crazy beliefs, ritual shunning, and tragic deaths is a look at a dying culture. In a time when it is common to talk about two Americas, I worry that we are talking about two realities. We can agree to disagree about whether or not there's a God, but we can't agree to disagree about whether or not I am possessed by an evil spirit.

All the Christian Truthers in this book believe in literal demonic possession. Many believe demons pop in and out of bodies, using the people around the target as hosts while they execute their torment. If you say I'm possessed, we don't have a difference of opinion. We're occupying two realities.

Plato's allegory of the cave in his *Republic* is supposed to praise the search for truth, but the line I borrowed at the beginning of this introduction has always been the takeaway for me. People want to be safe and comfortable in their beliefs and their lives. On the face of it, this is a story about when death is preferable to trading a certain reality for an uncertain one.

What follows is my account of and attempt to come to terms with both *what* happened and *why* things happened as they did. As loud as they tend to be, the old-time religions are dying, or at least changing. Reality is raining down upon them. Since so many people are seeking justification where none can be found in accepted reality, they've carved out their own—where the God of the Hebrews and science fiction cohabitate, and the truth is what you say it is.

1

HE SAID, "HERE! PRESS THIS HERE," OH, MY GOD!

Barbara Rogers stood screaming over the fresh corpse of Steven Mineo. The scene was too vivid, as if it were staged. Ignoring the brain matter on the bed, Barbara shook Steven again, begging him to wake up as she choked back another wave of panic. She wanted more than anything for him to get back up, to relive the last moments of his life, of their life together, and prevent this from ever happening. Maybe they had gone to bed as she wanted to, and she was just dreaming. Maybe this was one of the alternate realities Steven was obsessed with, and somewhere in another dimension none of this had happened.

She looked into his empty face, his head lolled back as if he were dozing, but his open eyes told a different story. The agony was gone, but so was the humor, the defiance, and the adoration they'd contained before the gun went off. She looked again at the fresh bullet wound in the middle of his forehead, and the screams returned. Barbara Rogers checked out.

The next few hours were just snapshots. A frantic 911 call telling the dispatcher that Steven had put the gun in her hands and then to his own head. "He said, 'Here! Press this here,' oh, my God!"

Steven's limp body as she looked around for the gun at the dispatcher's request, the foul smell of cramped living and gunpowder.

The patrolman coming around the corner, backlit by the blue and red lights of his cruiser in the humid, predawn Pocono Mountain summer.

Sitting handcuffed in the back of his cruiser, cuffs tight against her thin wrists, pinching and discomforting, as more police arrived.

The long, dark ride to the Pocono Mountain Regional Police Department as the sun threatened to break over the Pocono Mountains of eastern Pennsylvania.

Sometime after she was handcuffed and before her interrogation started, Barbara knew her old life was over, but she could not fathom why—only that it all started with Sherry Shriner.

*   *   *

The crime scene was a disaster, a homicide in the back room of a trailer that had been converted into a studio apartment. The victim, identified as Stephen "Steven" M. Mineo, a thirty-two-year-old New Jersey man who shared the space with the suspect, forty-two-year-old Barbara Hellen Rogers, sat on the floor, hands at his side, legs crossed at the calves, head back on the bed. The star-shaped powder burn around his head wound suggested the gun had been pressed against it, or at least quite close, before discharge.

Steven's bulletproof vest was open in the middle of the floor not far from his body. Given the close quarters, though, everything in the room was near the body, yet the room felt smaller than that. Steven and Barbara stuffed all their possessions into this space, piled high in closets and spilling from drawers, stacked on the cheap entertainment center, and in loose piles. Steven's phone was on the bed, silent.

There was evidence of heavy drinking in addition to a technically legal drug called Kratom. A bevy of prescription pills, some labeled, some not, all would be identified as Barbara's. In the yard, fewer than thirty yards from the scene, not far from the small wooded area the trailer bordered, police found four spent rounds. Five shots had been fired from the gun. There was a casing missing. On its face, this was a domestic incident gone wrong. One of them was cheating or leaving or being abusive, a handgun came out, end of story.

What the authorities didn't know at the time was this was the latest in a series of destroyed lives at the hands of Sherry Shriner, an internet preacher and rural Ohio housewife spreading hate, paranoia, and doomsday prophecy.

Sitting at her computer, the air stale with grease and cigarette smoke, Sherry commanded an army of thousands, each warrior desperate to fight in the impending War of Armageddon. Each assured they were under personal attack from the reptilian forces of the New World Order (NWO), and exhorted to take the fight to the enemy—the pop stars, actors, and world leaders who were secret lizard people bent on world domination.

The initial story, on the local news stations and in *The Pocono Record*, said a woman killed her boyfriend because he asked her to, claiming it was his only escape from Sherry Shriner's cult. According to police, Steven believed the cult leader had turned into a reptile. The fervor lasted a couple of weeks, getting legs from the bizarre and the clickable headlines it provided, many taking the form of "Man Begs to Be Killed to Escape Reptile Cult."

Think pieces about internet cults and the pervasive and ill effects of YouTube conspiracies rose and fell as they tend to in a media sensation's death throes. After all, the upshot was one crazy person killed another crazy person for no reason. It's a story with limited appeal. It certainly hadn't appealed to me.

I didn't get wind of Sherry Shriner for more than eighteen months after Steven's death, and even then it seemed like a shallow story. I was a freelance journalist searching for a story that was true crime-adjacent to turn into a podcast. I was developing one about religious scammers with a convoluted belief in the economic reset. I wasn't compelled by a guy who was in a crazy reptile conspiracy cult and got offed.

But what I would come to discover is that these weren't crazy people. They were part of a Christian subculture where aliens disguised as humans fight on the side of evil and New World Order cabals trade in pedophilia and mass cannibalism.

Followers accepted this for the same reason most of us believe whatever we believe—someone they trusted told them or personal experience did. It's less mental illness than an oversensitivity to disinformation. The people I've researched and spoken with are victims of a crumbling power superstructure, one where the old guard can't be trusted to uphold traditional morals and where government officials have dropped the pretense of public service. They are not wrong, but they can't cope with the banality of that truth.

I started looking into Steven's death in 2019. For more than a year, I was drawn into a world where the official story was always a lie. I spoke with people who I came to discover didn't just have fringe opinions but inhabited a different reality. One where Lucifer operates with impunity and his minions can possess or even replace any person at any time.

Among the thousands of pages and files in the court records, I discovered audio files. As it would turn out, Steven Mineo preferred to communicate by sending audio messages over Facebook Messenger. Many of his interlocutors followed suit. As a result, I got to hear their tone and the utter sincerity with which they professed their beliefs to one another. I listened, stunned, for hours.

When I stopped gawking at all the absurdities (and it was difficult to look away sometimes), I saw the lengths to which people go to protect their fragile reality and wondered how I would respond if someone tried to tell me that nothing I believed was true. Not just about God, but about my self-image and my experiences. I understood Sherry's followers were fighting like mad to keep from realizing theirs was a false reality, choosing instead to add layers of even less credible explanations than they'd begun with.

I learned about orgone, a powerful spiritual force the government doesn't want us to have, and about shapeshifters and clones (shapeshifters are individuals who can change their form at will). I learned how organized religion came to be under Satan's thumb and about the very real occurrence of spiritual warfare. Mostly I learned how one rural housewife with the sheer audacity to double down on every lie could make a small fortune baiting the lonely, gaslighting the paranoid, and ruining so many lives along the way.

2

I KNOW FULL WELL THIS IS CRAZY.

Kelly Marie Pingilley concentrated on Sherry Shriner's voice and kept typing. God only knows what time it was, not that it mattered. Kelly was a being outside of time. She knew that now. Sherry had taught her that. Everything in Kelly's life made sense now. The attacks, the years of torture in the bowels of hell, the inability to connect to her Lutheran community in any way.

Sherry knew all about it, had been through it, and came out on the other side anointed by Yahuah (God's real name, according to Sherry) for her fidelity. Kelly felt privileged to transcribe Sherry's radio shows, to listen closely and learn, sure, but to interpret as well. In some ways she was serving "Yah" through Sherry, but in other ways she was preparing for her own final transformation into an Angel in the Flesh.

Sherry Shriner's ministry was a machine that burned human fuel. Like so many others, it depended on a lot of donations and even more volunteer work. As her radio show gained popularity, Sherry made calls for transcription volunteers, people to help spread her word to those who couldn't or didn't stream the audio. The genius of this can't be overstated. It's only in the last few years that podcasts have started posting transcripts to improve their search engine results. The transcriptions drove Sherry's popularity, and Kelly transcribed dozens if not hundreds of her shows.

For most of her life, Kelly lived with her parents, her sister, Amanda, and her brother, Nate, in the Detroit suburb of Redford, Michigan. She was a quirky, silly, good-natured young woman, clear-eyed and fair-skinned with a tendency to comb her long brown hair in almost arrow-straight lines around her bangs, letting the rest frame her face and spill down her front. She looked younger than her twenty-two years, but not because she was petite as much as because she radiated energy, innocence, and enthusiasm.

Kelly devoted more than two years of her life to Sherry's cause, volunteering full-time as a Sherry Shriner evangelist. She believed with all her heart that the more people she exposed to Sherry's truth, the better. When she first stumbled upon Sherry's teachings, however, Kelly had no idea she would be the latest in a litany of rivals and acolytes Sherry burned through in her rise to greater and greater popularity.

Kelly arrived in Sherry's Facebook chat room the way so many others had, trying to reconcile the Illuminati, the NWO, aliens, and the Bible. She was bright and friendly, open to the new ideas she found as she started looking beyond her conservative Lutheran upbringing. To her, being more open-minded would help reconcile some of the questions she had about faith, salvation, and the end times.

Kelly was obsessed with being good from an early age. She'd confessed to her friend Rebekah Lasak that she needed to atone for her elementary school viciousness, to make an outward effort to be a better Christian, and to do more good. Long before she was fascinated by end-times prophecy, Kelly obsessed over all things soteriological. That is, she wanted to know the rules for getting into heaven, for being a good person, and for doing what God wanted of her. Religion was as much her entertainment as it was her ethical jumping-off point, and she believed the Bible contained answers for those willing to study and understand its hidden meanings.

Kelly's curiosity about salvation and punishment seemed to revolve around an innocent fascination with sex. When she began wondering whether someone who was close to her had been intimate with their fiancé, it terrified her. What if they died before they got married? Would they go to hell? What if they broke up? It was a simple and natural curiosity that devolved into an obsession that only darkened over time.

It's impossible to begin to comprehend the damage religious sexual prohibitions have done. There's emerging evidence that conspiracy theory obsession with child-trafficking is tied to child abuse among the ultra-religious. Unable to come to terms with abuse in their own backyards, they invent an evil other to blame. A healthy attitude about human sexual nature isn't part of the religious platform. As a result, there's a breaking point for young adults where rules about sex weighed against the threat of hell lose their force and become an obsession.

Just as Kelly obsessed about premarital sex, another friend, Marcy Walsh, struggled with her sexuality. She thought she might be attracted to girls which, as she had been taught since she was little, was a direct ticket to hell. As bright, curious students in a conservative Christian high school, looking for answers in the Bible just seemed natural. Kelly and Marcy were young and naive when they started having adult conversations and searching for biblical answers, and as they got older each found different answers to nebulous questions about life and morality.

Kelly was one of a foursome that included Rebekah, Britt Simpson, and Marcy in one of those deep and admirable friendships that transcends religious differences and doesn't rely on the past, but rather on a deep mutual affinity. These were four girls who leaned on each other as their worlds transformed, and relationships with their parents, other friends, boys, and spirituality became both more intricate and complex. All had serious adult-level struggles and felt as if they only had one another.

Rebekah lost her mother at the end of their freshman year of high school, Marcy struggled with her identity, and Kelly worried over her parents' failing marriage. Britt switched to a secular school before long where she had her own adjustment issues. Although Britt bailed on conservative religion, it didn't matter to the other three. They all leaned into nerd culture one way or another, each finding their preferred outlet, but they bonded over board games.

* * *

The Blue Roof Diner could've been a Howard Johnson's back in the 1970s, an A-frame-style building with peaked awnings above the side entrances. It's a classic suburban, alt-kid hangout situated along one of the arterial highways pumping sprawl from nearby Detroit. The girls would sit in a booth, playing euchre and occasionally succumbing to the perpetual aroma of coffee and French fries, the latter underdone, the former burned black, until all hours of the night. They were well-behaved kids too young to hit the bars, so this was a pleasant alternative to a night in any-one's parents' house. They came to the Blue Roof to laugh and to become better friends, and they succeeded every time.

Once, Kelly noticed an elderly man struggling with his meal. He was having trouble cutting his steak into small enough pieces. Kelly jumped up, crossed the aisle, and cut his entire dinner for him. She wasn't showing off or being giddy, just striving to help wherever she could, but it's notable how what Kelly saw as a self-imposed penance looked to everyone else like genuine Christian charity.

Although they drifted in their personal lives after graduation, each staring terrified into adulthood in her own way, the friendship endured beyond that summer of 2008. The next two years found Kelly drifting into a deepening depression. She'd done well in school but didn't head straight off to college. Kelly was trying to find herself and fought to come to terms with her parents' deteriorating marriage. Once her parents divorced, Kelly confided her relief to Rebekah and seemed to lighten after.

Kelly tried to be relentless in her optimism. She believed that if a person could act a certain way, they could achieve their goals, and her goal, it seemed, was making sure she got into heaven.

It's naive to dismiss the mystical aspect of prayer as any different from spells. Many people believe prayers said in the correct way, with the correct attitude and intention, can sway their deity. The more Kelly studied the Bible and researched and interpreted what it was purported to say about salvation, the closer she came to Sherry Shriner's orbit.

By 2010, she entered that mad gravity and would spend the rest of her life torn between the world she knew and the one she discovered. When Rebekah invited Kelly to come live with her in Adrian, Michigan, not far from Detroit, she'd already taken those first tentative steps into the mystical.

Rebekah had opened a Cutco cutlery distributorship, selling knives and hiring others to sell them as well. Cutco is a storied multi-level marketing (MLM) endeavor that's had distributors selling knives door-to-door for more than fifty years. Rebekah hired Kelly to work for her, and the pair moved into a small apartment that acted as a combination office/bachelorette pad.

Kelly had a car and no job, Rebekah had a job and no car, plus they were best friends and it was an adventure—a couple of twenty-somethings test-driving adulthood. This almost certainly is where Kelly crossed paths with Sherry Shriner for the first time.

Adrian is a small Midwestern city or a large Midwestern town. It has the traditional storefront-with-upstairs-apartments downtown, a Methodist college, and a struggling arts scene. As late as 2010, it had a video store where Rebekah and Kelly would stock up on movies to try and mitigate the bleak evenings. They weren't broke, but neither were they flush, and there was nothing for them in Adrian. Then, for the first time in their lives, Rebekah started butting heads with Kelly over religion.

Depression is a plague that grips some people worse than others, but it's an aspect of this story I always see lurking in the background. Even as I fight temptation to cast everyone involved as suffering from depression and to attribute everything that happened to this low, black, empty feeling, it bears acknowledging. Without casting too much aspersion Cutco's way, direct sales is a difficult and tenuous way to make a living, and it was all the girls had in their day-to-day lives, enduring long hours in the office followed by evenings in front of the television, watching whatever they could rent at the Adrian video store and waiting for bedtime.

Eventually, Kelly started breaking off a little early to go online, where she lost herself in Sherry Shriner's blogs and YouTube videos.

Sherry was a fan of the conspiracy website Vigilant Citizen and happy to co-opt its videos to spread her message. Vigilant Citizen is a website that spews NWO conspiracies. Proof that they are out to get you. It's garden-variety stuff, secret symbols in music videos, shadow police with superpowers kidnapping people in dark, grainy security footage. One thing that binds the conspiracy theory crowd is they don't collect evidence; they collect proof. I suspect many of them do not know the difference between the pieces and the puzzle.

Sherry didn't produce a lot of videos. Instead, she shared others' as if they were textbooks she would be lecturing on. It didn't matter whether she agreed with the person who made the video, only that there was a section in it she could point to and say, "This is what I had prophesized earlier."

Kelly watched rapt as Sherry explained how rich and powerful celebrities and international politicians had all been, or were going to be, replaced by reptilians after having their souls removed as part of Lucifer's end-times reign. Sherry would show how slow-motion video, sometimes from the Vigilant Citizen site, revealed skin moving on people's faces—a telltale sign they were reptiles wearing human suits.

Like a junior editor at the *Weekly World News*, Sherry highlighted "unexplainable" bruises and scars indicating recent soul scalping, the process by which reptilians replace a victim's soul. Using other people's YouTube videos, she also showed her followers how prominent backward masking (the messages you can hear if you play audio in reverse) and arcane symbolism are in popular culture.

Eventually Kelly introduced Rebekah to *Vigilant Citizen*, showing her the satanic symbolism in Lady Gaga. Rebekah blew it off as a case of a crackpot on the internet, but Kelly objected.

"I know full well this is crazy," Kelly said. "If I were you, I would also think this is crazy, but it's totally true."

What Rebekah would come to learn over those next weeks was that by "totally true," Kelly meant that the information had been confirmed by Sherry Shriner, but it would be much longer than that until they both learned that Sherry Shriner was a bald-faced liar and a religious con artist.

3

HEY, PASTOR, DID YOU EVER LOOK INTO THE REPTILES RUNNING THE WHOLE PLANET?

Sherry Coberly was born in 1965 and raised in a conservative religious household, which, as it would turn out, wasn't conservative enough for her.

Her father, Gary, worked as a salesman all of his life and spent a chunk of it as an active member of the Geauga County Republican Party, serving seven years as its chairman. Well-fed and ruddy, he's not a hard guy to imagine: avid golfer, knows people by name, comfortable making deals and compromises in his professional and personal lives, apt to loiter after church to greet his friends and neighbors and ask after their families.

Although Sherry attended church as well as Christian schools, by adulthood she came to hate the idea of organized religion, considering it a New World Order front bent on destroying the Word of God. This isn't uncommon among the conspiracy theory crowd. Such thinking has to do with a combined deep mistrust of authority and overconfidence in your own expertise. There's no point in trying to break apart this constant, low-level paranoia with logic; it's governed by fear and arrogance coalescing into a persecution feedback loop.

Insert here a bright and wily kid who gets a kick out of not just reading the Bible, but interpreting it, figuring out the real rules, and watching how deftly or poorly her elders deployed them. Sherry learned early in Baptist and evangelical circles that interpretation was a secret language where the speaker could finesse the rules to make a larger point. Revealed truth is just a matter of convincing people you're right and have the authority to wield truth. If nothing else, that was the insight she took with her to Liberty University in Lynchburg, Virginia, where she had designs on launching her quest to become a cable news star.

Later in her life, Sherry spoke fondly about working for Jerry Falwell, founder of the Moral Majority, the political movement that launched evangelicals into the national spotlight. She covered Falwell for *The Liberty Champion* and met him occasionally. There's no doubt she was impressed by him and influenced by his tactics. Beyond the paper, Sherry was involved with the radio station and in producing the yearbook. In photos, Sherry is the new face of the Christian right—the sharp tip of the new moral majority, unimpeachable and relentless.

It's easy to look at a photograph of someone when they're young and project the person they became onto them. It's also not fair choosing a few milliseconds out of two years of experiences and using them to paint a picture, but there's a marked difference between freshman year Sherry, posed to look angelic and hopeful in school-portrait grayscale, and the sophomore in the big-shouldered business blouse and slacks, formerly frizzy hair tamed into a gentle feather-back.

This Sherry is defiant, staring down the barrel of the camera with the rest of her newspaper staff. A jeer and a dare that belie the kind of mind that's always plotting revenge for insults real and imagined, but easily could be interpreted as self-assured and jocular. Fair or not, because Sherry published so few photos, they're always going to look indicative of the person she became.

People leave college after two years for lots of reasons, so it's pointless to guess what sent Sherry back to Ohio after her second year at Liberty in Virginia. When she talked about leaving Liberty University to go to Kent State, that's all she said on the matter in her website bio: "After two years in Virginia, I transferred to Kent State University where I was elected to become the director of their campus radio news department. During that time, I also took a job with a local newspaper focusing on political news. I graduated in 1991 with degrees in Criminal Justice, Journalism, and Political Science."

Sherry was at Liberty for the 1984–1985 and 1985–1986 school years, and said she took her degrees in 1991. Sherry was nowhere near as prominent at Kent State as she was at Liberty, and we'll have to take her at her word that she got all those degrees before she moved to Washington, DC, to get a job. And here, I can say with a little more confidence, she definitely couldn't cut it.

I can't imagine what life was like for a hard-core evangelical young woman who valued her own opinion and independence above all else. And that's today. Drop that person into the sexist atmosphere of 1990s DC journalism and it's not hard to see why she might get the opinion that the literal devil was running the country's capital.

Sherry variously said she left DC because she was called to higher things, because they gave her the runaround, and because they were all Satanists. I think she believed all of those things. There's no telling how she was treated there, but one assumes not well. Whether she landed an internship or an entry-level job, Sherry wasn't in a position of authority and could tell she never would be.

Sure, Sherry could have tried other cities and towns, which is the common way up in journalism. Two or three years in a small market and up and out from there, picking up experience and a better understanding of what counts as a source, as a lead, as evidence. Being a woman still would have been a huge hurdle all on its own.

Add in Sherry's sanctimonious, Bible-beating aura and a personality that took a scorched-earth approach to disagreements, and I think she knew she was a long shot in journalism. There's a certain way some people say "I'm a Christian" that implies they're one of the only Christians. That's how Sherry sounded to me. I think it was intentional.

Kent State isn't far from Ravenna, Ohio, where Sherry made her early married life with Arch Shriner. Today's Arch, gray-bearded and hollow-cheeked in the Facebook profile photo he took while looking down at the keyboard, wasn't at all interested in speaking with me except to say that everything I needed to know about Sherry was in her teachings. I couldn't tell if he was messing with me or not.

* * *

Let's look at NESARA, or the economic reset that is alleged to be a secret government plan to erase all debt that was foiled by, as well as the reason for, the 9/11 attacks. In reality, the National Economic Security and Recovery Act was a proposal by economist Harvey Francis Barnard in his manifesto, *Draining the Swamp: Monetary and Fiscal Policy Reform*. It proposed a lot of Libertarian ideas, including abolishing the income tax and returning to the gold and silver standards.

Barnard sent a copy, which included wording for the proposed bill, to every member of Congress, where it was ignored by all. For reasons that will forever be unclear, it was seized upon by thieves and charlatans, claiming God wanted his followers to invest in NESARA and would reward them with returns of as much as 500 percent.

When scams were busted by the authorities, many of the victims refused to come forward, seeing it as a government ruse to cut out the little guy from the big profits. To this day, thousands of people, maybe tens of thousands, believe NESARA was to be enacted on September 11, 2001, and the attacks on New York and the Pentagon were the NWO's last-ditch effort to stay the economic reset. This culture of fraud and deceit spread easily from mail-order scams to the internet in the 1990s, and likely introduced Sherry to the possibilities of online ministry riches. NESARA was a theme in her early shows. Either way, it wouldn't be long before Sherry dipped her toes into religious e-commerce.

If you have the fortitude and the luxury, it's easy to turn up your nose at get-rich-quick schemes and MLM plans. Yes, broadly speaking, they're a colossal waste of money, let alone time and effort, and prey upon people who can't afford them. Lottery tickets get the same bad rap for the same reasons. While the world would be a better place if people didn't scam one another, consider Sherry's state: a college-educated housewife living in, as she put it, "the backwoods of Ohio." She could have worked hard and become a retail manager, but that was her best-case scenario given her circumstances. If your odds aren't great for being able to work your way up and out, it makes sense on some level to drop a couple of dollars on the long shots along the way.

Trying to understand why Sherry got to where she did gave me an in. There are so many "whats" in this story, and they are all so tempting and bizarre. There are serpent seedlines, hollow planets where aliens hide, evil cabals at every level of government trying to kill a housewife in eastern Ohio. When it comes to Sherry Shriner's career, it's hard not to get distracted and enumerate the fantastical. The "whys" and "hows" of Sherry's ministry and the lives it crushed force us to squint against the sun of her audacity to even detect them. When we do, though, we'll have a better picture of how it got so bright.

If Sherry had a gift, it was her ability to convince people of the war Lucifer raged against her, personally, her whole life. It makes it tough to say with any confidence what is true about her origin story and what she reverse-engineered to fit her myth and her vanity. Most of Sherry Shriner's past is courtesy of Sherry herself, and it's all her followers know.

By tracing Sherry's claims between her spiritual dimension and real life, I felt something of a rising anger both at good people's astounding credulity and at Sherry's ability to exploit it without shame or mercy. For Kelly, the hook was orgone, a mystical energy that was a gift from God. Orgone became the placebo that kept Kelly's desperation, loneliness, and, most important, demons at bay.

Orgone would power Sherry beyond anything she could have dreamed. It helped her grow an empire capable of crushing individuals and ruining families, but Sherry already had cultivated her reputation as a prophet before she stole her orgone theories. In fact, Kelly was still in grade school when Sherry lit upon *The Bible Code* as a key to unearned wealth.

* * *

Journalist Michael Drosnin's book *The Bible Code* was a pseudo-academic work demonstrating that the "Jewish Books of the Bible" (meaning the Torah) could be used to reveal the future. It was based on a real scientific project wherein the Torah was laid out like a giant word find and investigators chose random patterns (the third letter on every fourth page, something like that).

To their shock, names like "Kennedy" and "Hitler" appeared. Criticism of the project reminded would-be prophets that any long work produced the same effect, but Drosnin ran with the debunked theory and even added his own twist.

An atheist, Drosnin didn't believe that God wrote the Bible. In his view, the book likely was authored by time-traveling aliens who left clues about our history for us to discover. It's a little amazing that an advanced species would take the time to jot down, say, the list of Adam's descendants or prohibitions against homosexuality. Still, I like his theory because it explains why we don't see the names and places involved with major events until after they happen, but people who took *The Bible Code* seriously took the hidden messages as prescriptive.

Sherry said God told her to buy *The Bible Code* computer program in 2001 (I would guess she bought it on Sept. 12, 2001). We know the events around the 9/11 attacks launched thousands of would-be doomsday prophets. The attacks begat the "Truther" movement (so named for the people who wanted to know the real truth about who was behind it all), which coalesced from far-flung corners of the internet before the fires in Lower Manhattan were out.

The events broke some people. I think we all know people who emerged from the fall of 2001 meaner and more afraid. By embracing the Truther movement, weak-minded people didn't have to deal with the complexities of cultural and geopolitical change. America still was invincible to attack by external forces, but the deep state had become too powerful.

One dominant political message was "Everything Has Changed." Another was "We Need to Get Back to Normal." I think that opened a rational disconnect for people and dragged religious thinking deeper into secular life. The attacks spread paranoia on a mass scale. It was a disease from which not everyone would recover. The Truthers made 9/11 their cornerstone; they grabbed onto that fear and held fast as if to their faith. Then it became their faith. Sherry Shriner was a participant in this emerging religion and also a beneficiary of it.

The early Truther movement attracted every stripe of spiritual practice across racial and cultural divides and even included atheists. It reflected a bizzaro, utopian America. The only requirement for inclusion in the group was the confidence that all government information is a lie aimed at furthering a secret agenda. The internet facilitated a new culture where Truthers could set aside their petty religious, ethnic, and racial differences and get to work proving that the 9/11 attacks were an inside job.

A new standard of proof emerged, and truth got a lot more slippery. Any explanation from an official source was a lie, but an explanation so crazy it just might be true had to be run down at any cost. The search for other worldwide cabals spread to become a magnetic hub around which frightening ideologies revolved, blended, and morphed. Think "the enemy of my enemy is my friend," where your primary enemy is the truth.

* * *

Sherry Shriner booted up her computer. A grid of Hebrew letters on digital parchment took up the center of the screen. She clicked on the search bar, blinking blue at the top, and began her keyword search. She typed out the words in English and the machine searched the Torah for her keywords in ancient Hebrew. Wherever they appeared, the program lit the letters and patterns up in red and blue. From there, Sherry had to divine how they related.

She threw herself at this new toy, discovering not only that she was God's Ambassador on Earth, but also a direct descendant of King David (of David and Goliath fame). It was revealed to Sherry that she'd been anointed to bring God's word to the people. Most important, *The Bible Code,* computer edition, revealed the alien agenda, the plan to replace all the world's most powerful people with reptilians and kill and clone those they couldn't soul-scalp.

I can picture thirty-something Sherry sitting in her cluttered kitchen, hunched over her computer, *Judge Judy* playing at a spectacular volume as she scrolled. She's dressed for the occasion, maybe in sweatpants and a baggy T-shirt, blondish hair drawn up and away from her puffy oval face, clipped just at the back of the top of her head. A cigarette burns in an ashtray, but never for too long without attention. More than a decade out of college, her four kids lurching toward adolescence, Sherry Shriner still hadn't hit the big time.

Then, a flash. A soaring-score, sunbeam-breaking-through-the-clouds moment of pure inspiration. Anyone could buy *The Bible Code*, but there's no way just anyone could use it. Sherry understood only someone anointed by God could understand the codes, as she called them. A simple dawning, sure, but also one that opened like a riddle you forgot you were struggling with, an intellectual "pop."

Sherry's first book, *Bible Codes Revealed: The Coming UFO Invasion*, chronicles God's encoded messages to Sherry, including her Davidic lineage, the hierarchy of angels, and the coming end of times. Where Sherry seemed to distinguish herself, though, was a novel interpretation on the relationship between Lucifer and the coming alien invasion.

In fundamentalist circles, what we think of as aliens are in fact demons. Sherry knew this. She also knew that Drosnin claimed the codes were written by aliens. Joining the dots, Sherry claimed aliens were fallen angels, Lucifer's generals and advisors, the shadowy beings who had tormented her throughout childhood. Demons were semi-corporeal beings in charge of possessions and mischief.

What Sherry called the alien agenda was a perfect entree for Truthers. Soldiers of Satan's army have infiltrated the government and other seats of power. Their agenda is to increase the world's evil and weaken its inhabitants, thereby making them unfit to serve in God's army. It's the original psy-op (psychological warfare operation): weaken support for God so he cannot muster a defense. This is why most traditional churches won't talk about the alien problem. They don't know. They're part of the power structure established by Lucifer at the time of Christ. Truthers believe that authority always lies. Who else always lies? The devil.

As the religious right continues to be absorbed into the Truther movement, there have been calls for pastors to protect their flocks from conspiracies, but it's a pointless exercise. Traditional religion won't have any more luck preventing the alien agenda than it does preventing premarital sex. The best it can do is drive it behind closed doors at the expense of active congregation members.

"Can you imagine going to your Baptist pastor and saying, 'Hey, Pastor, did you ever look into the reptiles running the whole planet?'" a long-time Shrinerite asked me. "Do you think they teach that in seminary?"

Sherry's followers believe they are in a literal war with the actual devil, like with armies and tactics and spies. They live in a world of magic where things are conjured by Lucifer to distract or disinform. I can't shake the feeling that the people who were disappointed when the world failed to end at the millennium were already on edge in 2001.

When the 9/11 attacks didn't usher in the War of Armageddon, it sowed a dangerous doubt. People faced the possibility that not only wasn't God coming, but maybe he wasn't there. Acknowledging that possibility throws some people's entire sense of self into question. Religious belief is their identity. It's something they'd die before losing, something they'd kill to keep. This isn't hyperbole, and the stranger the beliefs, the thinner the veneer. Sherry knew how to recruit from this group using social media and her weekly radio shows, and she knew how to keep them fighting for their beliefs.

There's a built-in persecution complex among fringe seekers. The feeling they somehow are prevented from getting the truth, that people don't want to answer their hard questions. But the simple case is there's nothing wrong with asking hard questions as long as you're willing to hear an answer. If you won't be convinced that the president isn't a reptilian in human skin, people are going to start avoiding you, and their avoidance is proof that you are onto something.

Sherry encouraged followers to switch their financial support from their own churches to her ministry. Churches were well-funded enough, she claimed, and many didn't know or care about the real truth. The living truth. The truth that God keeps anointing prophets, just not in the old churches. They're freelancers now, spreading their seed where it takes and shaking the dust from their sandals where it doesn't. Sherry's message was that God is still heavily involved, guiding his people daily and directing their actions based upon current events as they relate to his final plan. Plus, he had given them a divine weapon: orgone.

Sherry's thoughts and revelations about orgone don't appear until near the end of *Bible Codes Revealed*, although they occupied a central part of her ministry from the moment the book came out in 2005. The thing is, I'm not certain Sherry had even heard of orgone before she sat down to write.

4

YOU'RE A FUNDAMENTALIST FREAK SHOW, AND I'M NOT INTERESTED.

Wilhelm Reich claimed to have discovered orgone in the 1920s, but "invented" is more descriptive. This was a man driven by a glimpse of what he believed to be the truth, but he was a psychiatrist, not a physicist, so he had a different method of testing and standard of proof.

Reich was deputy director of Freud's Vienna Ambulatorium and did enduring work linking sexual repression and psychosis. Much of what we believe about the two comes from his insight and research. His professional successes gave him the confidence and drive to search for a universal cure for sexual repression, but, in that search, Reich lost touch with science and spun headlong into mysticism.

He posited that the serene sense of well-being associated with an orgasm was the result of tapping into an elemental force like gravity. He named the force orgone and commenced work on ways of harnessing and focusing this new energy. The more he looked into repression and orgasms, the more certain he was that he could design a system for harnessing and releasing the post-orgasmic sense of well-being without inducing an orgasm. Reich's obsession with this hidden power clouded his mind, and he confused genuine discovery with wishful thinking.

Reich was a trained psychiatrist, but there is a world of difference between a doctor and a physicist. Physicists try to describe why things have to happen the way they do. Their results must be exact and repeatable to count as successful. It's a distinction Reich ignored. If humans could be negatively affected by, say, ultraviolet radiation, it stood to reason they could be positively affected by orgone energy.

Perfecting the collection process became his life's work and eventual undoing. In 1939, Reich fled the war in Europe for the United States. By then he had been obsessing over and experimenting with orgone and its effects for two decades.

By the time he landed stateside, Reich already had designed and constructed a box he claimed could collect orgone energy. Lined with copper and crystals, Reich claimed the orgone accumulator created a greenhouse effect where orgone was trapped and amplified. The box was large enough for an adult to sit in comfortably, basking in the quiet, absorbing orgone energy, and improving their mental and physical health.

Reich went to Princeton where he met with Albert Einstein and pitched him his orgone theory. Einstein was said to be intrigued, and maybe that's true. He agreed to examine the orgone accumulator to confirm and explain the abnormal energy readings Reich had documented. A lab assistant debunked Reich's measurements almost at once, citing a basic physics principle. Reich and Einstein were done. And this is how science and religion part ways.

Confronted with indisputable evidence that orgone couldn't be measured by the primitive standards of his time, Reich came to understand orgone as an intuitive force. It became critical to be able to "feel" orgone energy. The accumulator worked, everyone who used it said so. It was up to the physicists to explain why.

Reich had more pressing matters, like the specter of the recent Dust Bowl in the American West. The United States government was funding research into preventing or even eliminating droughts, and Reich proposed a solution: orgone blasters—

35

massive pipes that focused orgone energy and could be used as a rainmaking apparatus.

Reich drove all over the West with his "cloud-bursting" device during the war years, trying to make it rain. His funding dried up, but Reich had what he needed, and what his acolytes cling to still: the legitimacy of having done government-backed research.

Today, orgone proponents claim that the government feared the power of orgone (this is the same government that was testing the atomic bomb) and initiated a smear campaign to discredit Reich and his discovery. After failing to sell his rainmaker to the government, Reich started hyping orgone as a cure for cancer, selling orgone accumulators to the desperate and the dying. The FDA told him to stop, and when he refused, they sent him to prison where he died in 1957. The end.

Among orgone's true believers, Reich's biography goes like this:

Wilhelm Reich discovered orgone, a secret energy source that is connected to everything. He developed it for the government and tried to share it with the world. Albert Einstein himself examined the orgone accumulator. When they discovered what it could do, the New World Order and Big Pharma had to make sure this cure-all didn't get into the public's hands. They ordered the police to storm Reich's offices, destroy his orgone accumulators, and burn all of his books to prevent his discoveries from getting out. Then they railroaded Reich and had him assassinated in prison.

The story isn't a lie so much as it's a conspiracy theory interpretation. Working backward from the conclusion that orgone is real and works, the rest follows naturally. Given that its inventor was jailed as a fraud, someone lied about the orgone accumulator's efficacy. Why would anyone lie? Because they have more to gain from the deception than they do from the truth.

Attempting to reverse-engineer facts from beliefs is the kernel of conspiracies from aliens to pharmacology. So many people are just doing their best to feel as if they're part of an intellectual endeavor rather than parroting received wisdom like the rest of us. Reich and the many orgone promoters who followed him thought of orgone as an instrument of peace and balance. Once Sherry Shriner got her hands on it, it became a weapon of righteous war.

* * *

Secular holy man Don Croft and his wife, Carol, were among the biggest names in orgone before Sherry came along.

Don Croft discovered the power of orgone in the 1990s. Like many conspiracy theory enthusiasts, Croft believed that chemtrails—the condensation trails left behind high-flying airplanes—were in fact poison gases released in the air.

Croft suffered his first bout of chemtrail poisoning while on a trip to California. He tried orgone out of desperation and found it cured his chemtrail sickness as well as dispelled his depression. Learning about Wilhelm Reich and understanding that the miracle could be conjured, Croft crafted "orgone zappers"—small boxes resembling magnetic key-hiders that contained crystals and produced a magnetic field. The outside had two large copper buttons that transmitted the orgone. They were an improvement on orgonite pucks, which were copper, crystals, and metal filings baked into cupcake-shaped resin.

Tall and broad, Croft had a high forehead, low eyebrows, and a deceivingly handsome face that looks immediately familiar. He could be the awkward but charming neighbor in a sitcom. He was a natural salesman. He began selling zappers and claimed to have been to Africa where he used them to cure malaria and AIDS.

They could be placed on sore joints or over general problem areas. The big breakthrough for him, though, was realizing that orgonite could heal the environment.

Croft believed cell towers put out negative ethereal energy, poisoning the surrounding air and water with bad vibes responsible for everything from foul weather to cancer. It's part of the paranoid radio waves lineage that moves people to wear tinfoil hats. As Truther culture has grown, so has terror of cell towers, but even back in the 1990s, Croft wasn't saying anything novel when he claimed cell towers needed to be neutralized. After the turn of the century, though, he found a way to marshal an army to attack the problem at the source.

"Gifting" was the process of setting orgonite (pucks or zappers, as the gifter preferred) around a cell tower's perimeter where the positive orgone energy (POE) could filter out the bad vibes. Croft reached out to the cell tower-fearing community to tell them about his discovery. He began speaking at alternative holistic health conferences, writing web articles, and making YouTube videos.

Because of his innovation in making orgonite zappers, he became the go-to authority on how orgonite worked, the science behind it, and different ways it could be used to purify. He encouraged everyone who hated cell towers to buy or make orgonite and share their gifting experiences with the larger community. His work resulted in an online forum celebrating gifting triumphs. Some users even posted video of guerilla actions involving orgoning cell towers.

For Croft, though, the gifting program was the breakthrough. Concerned citizens could do their part to dampen or even undo a tower's ill effects, even as corporations continued placing them strategically. Orgone zappers were open source by design. Making them was much more time-consuming and complex than making orgonite pucks.

If Croft had tried to become a sole provider, people would have lost interest quickly. By encouraging a new marketplace, Croft created a built-in supply-and-demand cycle where people would buy or make orgonite relics, throw them into the woods, and buy or make more. The market exploded. People from all over the world started gifting orgone and basking in the online glory of praise from what came to be called the Etheric Warrior community. After the Twin Towers strike on 9/11, Croft gained more influence and popularity as people sought new protections and weapons against shadowy threats they knew were out there but couldn't define.

The Etheric Warriors had a quasi-MLM structure with the more popular producers referring requests to lower ones on the totem pole. Scores of internet forums popped up (and remain) with advice on how to improve your orgone production. People on those sites formed loose affiliations and then tighter ones.

The critical difference between being an Etheric Warrior and, say, an Amway distributor is there wasn't a buy-in per se. All you had to do to sell orgone was start making it and let people know that you were gifting. And you didn't have to buy or sell orgone at all. You could just make your own orgone and gift it whenever and as often as you wanted.

It's easy to see the appeal. Orgone decentralized metaphysical power. You didn't need a blessing or a prayer from some minister. Anyone could capture orgone energy. Anyone could disperse it. Everyone controlled the manufacture and distribution of this occult power. And there was a social component. Some people bowl, some people golf, and some people go on trips around the country gifting orgonite to the areas where people didn't have the good sense to do it themselves.

Having a higher calling and going on missions makes people feel important. Plus, the more who join, the more POE is generated. It's almost utopian. People believed that, with enough orgone, they could undo the spiritual and the environmental damage cell towers, chemtrails, and electromagnetic field radiation (from home electronics) have caused to the planet.

From the outside, throwing special rocks at a piece of technology you don't understand seems primitive, but the enthusiasm is undeniable. After the turn of the century, the Etheric Warriors forum was alive and active with people of all stripes trying to find out how best to harness this power. This is almost certainly where Don Croft first came to the attention of Sherry Shriner.

Sherry reached out to Croft in 2004 while working on *Bible Codes Revealed*. She was cultivating a Yahoo Group following of hardcore conservative Truthers and preppers (survivalists preparing for social and political upheaval) drawn to her because she had the prophetic gift. God had led her to call upon Croft to join the mission.

According to *The Bible Code,* she said, Don Croft also was an important prophet and leader. Since he wasn't a Christian, Croft didn't even know he had been doing God's work. Sherry had seen it. Orgone was a gift from God, a shield from demonic attacks, and a sword against evil.

Sherry proposed they team up, offering access to her not-un-impressive Christian following as a sweetener. She told Croft her followers would be a huge boost to the Etheric Warrior base. Imagine having the audacity to reach out to a person who is more successful than you and offering to take some success off their hands.

Don wasn't having it. Geoff Brady, host of alternative radio show *In Other News,* which covers conspiracy theory news, summarized Don's response: "He said, 'No thanks,' You know? 'You're a fundamentalist freak show, and I'm not interested.'"

When he told me the story about Sherry and the Crofts, Geoff sounded a little offended that Sherry, still a really small-time player in 2004, had the audacity to even approach a heavy-hitter like Don Croft with such a transparent proposal.

Since Don was agnostic and Carol practiced earth-based spirituality, it's no shock they didn't want to get involved with Sherry and her doomsday prophecy followers. But Sherry's followers weren't turn-the-other-cheek Christians, they were burn-the-witch Christians, actively trolling and attacking unbelievers online and spewing the kind of hate you can imagine turning violent.

The Crofts wanted to protect the planet and its people from harmful technology, to reduce crime and sickness for everyone through orgonite. Sherry wanted to weaponize it for the coming War of Armageddon, and she didn't take "no" well.

When *Bible Codes Revealed: The Coming UFO Invasion* came out the following year, in 2005, Chapter 12 ("Tearing Down the NWO Strongholds: Orgone as a Self Defense Weapon") recounted Sherry's story of how God had revealed the history and power of orgone to her through the codes. The final appendix in the book was "How to Make Orgone Blasters."

At every opportunity, on her blog, her radio show, her Yahoo Groups, Sherry declared Carol a witch and Don, because of his process and his character, a purveyor of negative orgone energy.

When I asked him about it, Geoff bristled at the notion. Orgone was, by definition, positive energy that countered other negative energies. Claiming there was such a thing as negative orgone energy was as nonsensical as debating wet electricity. Sherry's attacks on the Crofts didn't endear her to the wider orgone-making community either. The idea behind orgone was to build a larger community; it didn't have to be a winner-take-all proposition.

What Geoff didn't quite get is Sherry couldn't leave the Crofts alone. She needed an enemy to rally her troops. She also needed a scapegoat for the orgone myth she constructed. In many conservative Christian circles, idolatry is strictly forbidden. No statues, no crosses, and no crystals under any circumstances. Sherry circumvented that by consulting *The Bible Code* and learning the true history of Wilhelm Reich and orgone.

Reich was only the latest in a long line of prophets and truth-tellers to whom God had revealed orgone, Sherry said. Orgone was used in ancient Egypt among the Chosen People for healing and protection. Reich had gotten too close to revealing the whole truth, though, so the NWO co-opted orgone by making things like orgonite zappers and other New Age crystals that transmitted evil into the world. Just as churchgoing Christians had been fooled into worshipping Satan, so too had Etheric Warriors been playing for the wrong side.

Sherry's solution, which played out over another two years and was detailed in her second book of 2005, *Aliens on the Internet*, was to warn people about who made Yah's orgone and who didn't. When people asked, and often when they didn't, Sherry would rant about how much damage the Crofts were doing with their worthless, evil orgonite zappers, and how inferior they were to her orgone blasters.

By 2007, Don Croft must have had enough because he wrote a blog post/open letter exposing her as a double-dealer. In the letter, Don said blowing off Sherry drew the attacks against his wife; it had nothing to do with his orgonite. He recounted the way she contacted him, offering to trade her followers for access to his. It's a letter tinged with righteous anger, but it didn't do any good.

While Croft did his best to ignore Sherry and stay true to his mission, Sherry was a recruiting machine. She spent her time cultivating a significant presence as an orgone purveyor and one of the go-to authorities on the subject. Don remained a major voice in the New Age orgone community until his death in 2017, but Sherry made it Christian, infuriating and undermining him in one easy go. Witches bought from Don Croft, but Christians would only use Sherry Shriner's orgone.

It was her first major conquest. Her orgone warriors were making and spreading orgone as a central piece of their practice. Just as Don had been early on, Sherry nearly was buried in orders and had to start outsourcing. She made videos about how to make what she called "Yah's Orgone" so people had access to her exacting specifications. Like any other spell, charm, or superstition, getting each step perfect was crucial to generating POE rather than NOE (negative orgone energy). And Sherry rarely missed the opportunity to plug orgone gifting missions during her sometimes thrice-weekly radio shows:

> The chemtrail planes come, they spray, nothing sticks, they leave, because the orgone keeps chemtrails from staying in your area. And so what they're gonna do is unleash their chemtrails, and what we're gonna do is keep pounding the orgone out there, getting it out there more and more, to fight against their chemtrails.

5

SHERRY GIVES A LOT OF TRUTH.

For Kelly Pingilley, orgone was a godsend. Not only did Sherry experience night terrors like her and doubt whether the traditional church had any answers in the same way she did, but Yah had told Sherry Shriner his real name and revealed to her a way to defend against all the black, awful beings set on her destruction. As it was for thousands of other people, Sherry's prophecy was the catch, but her orgone was the hook. Once she understood how alike she and Sherry were, Kelly wanted nothing more than to be an orgone warrior.

Kelly was already being drawn into Sherry's life when she went to live with Rebekah in Adrian, Michigan, but she wasn't yet "out" as a Shrinerite. Instead, Kelly would spend her downtime scrolling through Sherry's writings, listening to and transcribing her radio show, and developing a spectacular understanding about the prophet and her teachings.

Kelly had been plagued with night terrors for years and felt a kinship with Sherry, who said she had been haunted by monsters from birth. These dark, looming creatures, who by Sherry's account were the inspiration for Darth Vader, would stand at the end of her bed at night, menacing. Little Sherry Coberly would lie beneath her covers, pressing her eyelids tight and praying to God that the monsters would leave. They did, only to return the following night and repeat the cycle. This happened for her entire childhood until she realized she was protected by God and could dispel the monsters in his name.

"Night terrors are real," Sherry wrote of the experience. On the face of it, that's not an outrageous claim. I think we all accept that night terrors are real. What Sherry meant, though, was these were alternate realities creeping through tears in time and space. Realities where demons were real and had power. Realities where awful, awful things happened. The explanation appealed to Kelly.

This is how otherwise well-intentioned bright people find their way into Sherry's web. They find one thing that clicks and grab onto it for dear life. Her followers use phrases like "Sherry's truth" or "Sherry gives a lot of truth," and I get what they mean. If a person believes in hell and is terrified of going there, they also know there's not a lot of room for error when it comes to biblical interpretation.

Like a practiced mentalist, Sherry casts a wide, vague net, and people who are desperate for confirmation of a spirit world grab on and hold tight, molding their experiences to Sherry's prognostications. The more she gets right, the more authority she has.

Kelly did a deep dive into Sherry Shriner's teachings, first believing what she found and, over time, improving upon Sherry's teachings where possible. After she learned all she could about orgone from Sherry, Kelly researched the other esoterica the prophet shared, excited as she found answers about evil in the world and the coming apocalypse that finally made sense.

Kelly had learned as a little girl, for instance, that Lucifer led a failed rebellion against God and was cast into the pit of fire along with his accomplices. These were the demons and other evil creatures of myth. Sherry said they were not cast into the pit, but went to earth and started mating with animals, creating the races of hybrids that we think of as monsters. The Egyptian gods are among these, as are giants, zombies, witches, vampires, and the like. Sherry preached that these were real, though hidden, protected by government cover-ups and a complicit clergy.

Kelly read, bleary-eyed and fascinated, her agile mind filling in the gaps in Sherry's mediocre, slapdash storytelling. She read about the Serpent Seedline, the direct descendants of the unholy coupling of Lucifer with Adam's first wife, Lilith, before the Fall of Man, and more and more of it made sense. Kelly must have been astonished to learn that Paul the Apostle, who wrote much of the New Testament, was in truth an agent of Satan, deceived on the road to Damascus and enlisted to spread false doctrine.

Kelly was raised in Lutheranism, went to religious school and church on Sunday, but had never heard about the Book of Enoch, one of the apocryphal books of the Bible. Held as holy writ by several Christian sects today, it details the Fall, including how good and evil angels walked among man. Kelly became fascinated with the possibility that she was one of these creatures, what Sherry called an Angel in the Flesh, an eternal being in human form charged with fighting in the War of Armageddon.

Sherry conferred the title Angel in the Flesh upon her favorite followers through communion with a woman called Beverly Nelson, who was an upper-echelon Shrinerite. Among the other followers, it was whispered that Bev was a massive donor, providing Sherry with a shocking amount of financial support. She was without question an authority, though, and the person Sherry designated to inform acolytes if they were indeed an Angel in the Flesh. It wasn't the kind of honor a person could claim on their own.

The first time Kelly's roommate Rebekah tripped over an orgone puck outside of her bedroom door, Kelly explained that it protected them from evil spirits. Rebekah believed in the power of prayer, which she understood as the only thing necessary to secure God's blessings and protection. Orgone pucks were unnecessary. Kelly demurred, but continued leaving the stones and began trying to pray over Rebekah before they went to bed.

Rebekah was uncomfortable enough that she started varying her bedtime to undermine the ritual.

What neither could know at the time was that Kelly was slipping into a place of paranoia from which she wouldn't return. It was one of the first instances of Kelly choosing Sherry's teachings over the company of her family and friends, but it wasn't the last.

*   *   *

Kelly sat quietly in the therapist's waiting room. On the other side of the door, she heard Rebekah's muffled tones, not so much eavesdropping as unable to stop from listening. Kelly heard her name. Rebekah was complaining to her therapist about the nighttime prayers and the orgone she kept finding all over the apartment. Rebekah was asking her therapist for help finding a tactful way of getting Kelly to stop pestering her with conspiracy nonsense.

"I heard you in there," Kelly said, breaking the awkward silence on the drive home. Rebekah let it pass. She was embarrassed and guilty for hurting her friend's feelings. But she also was in therapy to work at exorcizing her own demons and more relieved than anything else she wouldn't be subjected to Kelly's conspiracy nonsense anymore.

Kelly was resigned. She'd been studying the Book of Job and had begun to feel a connection to that biblical character. In the Book of Job, God bets the devil that Job can't be turned against the Lord, and to demonstrate the point, God invites Lucifer to do anything he wants to Job, short of killing him. The devil proceeds to torture Job, killing his children, taking his land, visiting all manner of horrors upon him. Job doesn't break, instead he comes to learn that the more punished you seem, the more favored you are by God. Eventually, the Lord had enough and declared himself the winner. He blessed Job, who became financially successful, got a new wife, had lots more kids, and lived to be 140 years old.

This is what Kelly clung to as she prepared for her coming ordeals. Her friends would abandon her over her beliefs, and, like Job, she would be tortured beyond her ability to conceive pain, and then God would redeem her and restore her life better than it had been before. This is something she couldn't explain to Rebekah, that Rebekah couldn't understand even if Kelly tried.

Kelly had begun to suspect she might be an Angel in the Flesh. She started a blog called FirstFruits under the name Warrior Elect, which suggested both her status as an orgone warrior and as one of the 144,000 people who were born already saved, according to Revelations.

If what she suspected was true, she was responsible to fight in God's army in the War of Armageddon. Rebekah wouldn't understand the responsibility or accept that Kelly was right now living a secret life, fighting aliens and interdimensional beings, and dispatching MK Ultra agents (products of a government mind-control, super soldier program). Kelly kept her vocation to herself, but it didn't prevent her from walking the walk when it came to home security. After all, Angels in the Flesh are under near-constant attack by Lucifer, who hopes to keep them from fulfilling their duty.

* * *

Remember, these are kids in their late teens and early twenties. Their daily struggle with their own lives and futures consumed much of their thought. None of Kelly's friends had the experience or even the vocabulary to help.

What Kelly wanted to explain, if only she thought Rebekah could understand, was that as the end of the world approached,

Satan was getting stronger, and prayer alone might not be enough. The orgone warriors had to rise up and take part in the fight. It wasn't just a war between good and evil for dominance, but a war between the forces of good and the forces of evil for the safety and salvation of unclaimed souls—what the Shrinerites refer to as The Bride.

God wasn't coming to vanquish evil; his army was. Kelly Pingilley saw herself as a general in that army. She had seen spiritual battle and come through it.

6

WE WERE ALL ANGELS WITH MISSIONS.

Sherry posted a plea under the headline, "Government Stole My Orgone—Planning to Make Plane Explode and Blame it on My Orgone." In August 2011, God told Sherry that Mayor Rahm Emanuel was planning to shut down Chicago's O'Hare International Airport and stage a terrorist attack, blowing up an airplane. In the ensuing investigation, she said, the government would claim that orgone was the reason for the crash and use the opportunity to ban the dangerous substance.

Sherry used this story to encourage her followers to donate to her ministry and finance a much-needed orgone mission to the Windy City. She also needed volunteers to help place enough orgone around the airport that they wouldn't be able to crash a plane there. The cost of the orgone alone for a mission like this, she said, could run $4,000. That's $4,000 worth of resin, crystals, metal filings, and copper wire.

Kelly Pingilley was always up for an orgone mission. Because she was young and unattached, she volunteered often. Her friends would find out after the fact that she had been to different parts of the country on orgone missions. Such trips offered her a reason to explore the country, to do and see things she otherwise might have skipped or dismissed as frivolous reasons to travel.

Having a mission was critical for Kelly. Missions kept her life organized. They let her prove to herself time and time again that she was here for a reason, that her actions had far-ranging and positive import. Chicago was one of several cities Kelly went to at Sherry's behest. The prophet herself didn't make the trip in the fall of 2011, but she lauded the warriors who did without naming names.

Friends variously described Kelly as having gone to states out west as well as throughout her native Midwest. The only orgone mission she was on for which I have rich detail from multiple people was what I think of as the Battle of Fort Knox. It involved the real-world trip and supposed supernatural conquest of an alien base as well as the people who would become major players in Kelly's life, and then in Steven Mineo's.

* * *

There were agents on the lake. Richard Brown knew they had to be. A storm was coming in, and no one fishes during a thunderstorm. He motioned to the party, urging caution as they crept to the water's edge, launching orgone pucks into the water, and placing them in strategic positions near the shoreline.

A little farther along the shoreline, Richard brought them to a halt again. He identified a reptilian guard trying to thwart the mission. For those of us in this reality, what Richard saw looked like a Black man enjoying an afternoon near a peaceful lake, but Brother Rich, as he was called, was a veteran warrior and one of the prophet's regular traveling companions. He knew better.

Brother Rich reached into his shirt and pulled out an orgone pendant and held it up for the interloper to see. The man smiled and waved and moved on. For Brother Rich and the assembled, the man's retreat was proof that he was an agent spying on Sherry and waiting for a sabotage opportunity.

Brother Rich, Sherry, Marianne Mulloy (a shrill Shriner evangelist and one of Sherry's closest advisors), and another warrior I believe to have been Kelly were gifting orgone pucks in western

Ohio during this encounter. This was the first leg of the journey that would end in the Battle of Fort Knox.

The codes warned Sherry about a DUAB (Deep Underground Alien Base) beneath where all the gold in the US used to be. She was moved to go to Kentucky with her best orgone warriors and destroy it. As the group approached Fort Knox unmolested under the protection of God, they saw horrors that would keep them up nights. There was a huge brain in a jar and reptilian overlords torturing turtle people who had been brought in as slaves. Using orgone pucks and orgone blasters, Sherry and her team destroyed the base and rescued the turtle people, who were grateful and thanked them for their help.

Sherry told that story a couple of times. So did Kelly, Brother Rich, and Marianne. It's canonical lore among the Shrinerites. It keeps me up nights. I'm going to come right out and say I don't think it happened that way. I don't doubt they went to Fort Knox and orgoned the hell out of the place. But turtle people? Brains in jars? Maybe I'm oversimplifying, but given that there is no way the battle took place, why would they all describe it the same way?

I think back to being a child, role-playing army or cops and robbers, narrating the enemy's action aloud so my buddies could respond to and continue the narrative. I might just suffer from a dull imagination, but there was no reality attached.

I imagine it's the same for people who participate in live role-playing, dressing up like medieval soldiers and hitting one another with swords or blunted arrows. The battle is real enough, and the orcs or whatever are real enough for the fantasy, but not so much that any participant would later brag about having murdered an orc, human, or halfling.

Sherry didn't claim these were visions or that they entered the spirit realm for this battle (which would somehow sit easier with me). She claimed a group of otherwise nondescript individuals broke into a secret alien base under Fort Knox and fought monsters. I can only speculate about why the rest would perpetuate that lie, but it seems to be a comment on Sherry's power.

Throughout her career, Sherry pushed some of the most audacious lies onto her believers, demanding they accept them and repeat them back to her. I suspect it was partly a test, a way of securing allegiance and implicating them at the same time. Sherry constantly dared people to dissent and crushed them when they did. Fort Knox may have been part of that myth-building.

Kelly may have gone along with the story as if staying in character. It was an honor to be allowed to volunteer for Sherry, doubly so when God's Ambassador on Earth came on the mission herself. Kelly believed in orgone's power to save the planet from destruction and its inhabitants from hell. She believed in this outward sign of her higher calling to serve and protect in God's name. There was no way Kelly would jeopardize future invitations by not noticing the turtle creatures Sherry pointed out. At first, anyway. Before too long, though, Kelly would rise above Sherry's petty missions and assert herself as the person God needed to help save humanity's soul.

Brother Rich noticed they were being followed back to their motel after the Battle of Fort Knox. He and Marianne were in the chase car while Kelly and Sherry took point. A car had come up behind them as they made their quick right turn. The person in the car began honking the horn and swearing at them. Just as with the reptilian by the lake, two realities collided. In this case, a minor case of road rage became proof the New World Order was out to kill orgone warriors wherever they could find them.

It was all old hat to Brother Rich, who once absorbed an energy ray blast meant for Sherry that had left him sick for days. Learning to fight through the attacks was what being an orgone warrior was all about.

As Sherry's resident scholar, Brother Rich researched connections and cabals most people didn't even think to look for. His success in this, as well as his uncanny ability to cite biblical text and Sherry's own prophesies, presented as quiet vanity. It endeared him to Sherry, and in the insular Shriner household he was known as Uncle Rich, which stoked his ego all the more.

Beyond helping produce Sherry's radio shows, Brother Rich was happy to help out with chores Sherry's husband, Arch, didn't or wouldn't do, and to lavish praise, respect, and attention on Sherry as the pair sat out in her driveway watching spaceships burn up as they tried to enter the atmosphere over Sherry's house.

After Fort Knox, though, something changed. Sherry had discarded him, opting instead for Kelly, whose writing was straying more into commentary on Sherry's teachings than the reposting of them. Brother Rich was proud when Sherry called him her navigator, but now she had a new navigator.

When Sherry announced an orgone mission to New York City in August 2012, Richard elected not to go. He was beginning to get suspicious of Kelly's motives and of how close she was getting to the prophet.

* * *

The trip to New York was a massive success. Kelly navigated only insofar as she had the map. Sherry joked about how they got lost and turned around. Sherry's erratic driving and Kelly's half-step-behind map reading encouraged a sitcom atmosphere as they tooled around Manhattan. Sherry said that they never were lost, only detoured by God who was directing them to places where they could vanquish reptilians and void Lucifer's agents. God directed Sherry, and Sherry directed Kelly.

When Hurricane Sandy spared much of Manhattan that autumn, Sherry took the credit. Kelly didn't get a mention. Orgone warriors are nameless, mythical as their missions. This might have been Sherry's own vanity, but it's useful to think about it as a marketing ploy. Mentioning the active warriors by name put a number on it. Crediting "all" the orgone warriors who helped execute these missions made them legion. The fact that every mission prevented the event Sherry foretold only made her more credible.

When I was a kid, my mother would feign the ability to change traffic lights from red to green. Whenever we were rushing, she pretended not to understand my request to change the light until we'd been sitting for a while or she'd say she couldn't use that power all the time. These plausible distractions convinced me she had psychic powers for well longer than it should have.

Once we've decided we believe in something, it takes much more effort to un-believe than it does to take that belief a little further. In my case, I only stopped believing my mother was psychic (and telling my friends as much) after her trick was made clear. I didn't make an effort to debunk it, but rather held that belief until it was dismantled for me.

Orgone missions were Kelly's way of reinforcing the object's power and efficacy. Among her family and friends, she tried to pretend she wasn't terrified of the monsters and demons who were out to get her. On an orgone mission, she accepted the fact and took the fight to the evil surrounding her.

Her friends think she was obsessed with orgone, but it seems more subtle than that. Kelly honestly believed there was a war coming, but she didn't fear for her life or for her soul. Kelly had been designated as one of the 144,000 people who would be saved to fight in God's army, so her salvation was assured. But her friends? Her family? Theirs was not.

I don't think Kelly was obsessed with orgone so much as obsessed with protecting her loved ones once the apocalypse started. Also, at first blush, Sherry's religion didn't strike her friends as that crazy. Just as with Rebekah at first, Kelly's friend Britt didn't think it was dangerous or even unpleasant to learn about.

"The first time she explained it to me had to have been the way it was explained to her," Britt told me. "Because it actually made some sense at first."

Britt liked talking about spirituality. Even though she wouldn't describe herself as religious, she had a healthy metaphysical curiosity. Kelly told her how fallen angels had mated with animals to create what we now think of as the Egyptian gods, which is as enticing an explanation as any. Even as Kelly moved into the Illuminati, Britt was still almost on board. The idea that the government and corporations are lying to protect their secret agenda is always going to get a little traction. Kelly lost Britt with the reptilians and the alien agenda.

The Illuminati is one of Sherry's other reliable hooks because from there it's not too far a leap to reptilian overlords. That seems to be the dividing line. Britt said she knew there was corruption everywhere but wasn't willing to go the extra mile of assigning it to an ancient cult bent on world domination.

* * *

Kelly had the absolute faith in her orgone that many people have in the Christian cross or any other religious talisman. Maybe more so because there were monsters in Kelly's reality. Like many other Shrinerites, she believed addiction or mental illness was just possession. Rather than let the NWO-backed pharmaceutical industry pump more poison into you or, God forbid, implant a

6 We were all angels with missions.

chip, the best way to deal with demons of all kinds was to wear orgone at all times.

Sherry's ministry relied on self-reported miracles—incidents that proved Sherry was right. Kelly had one not long after she started wearing the orgone pendant, as she wrote in a testimonial on Facebook:

> I didn't really get a reaction from it at first or see just how much it was protecting me until I took it off at my work one day to hold it under some cold water, you know, to "clean" it. I work at a detox/rehab drug & alcohol rehabilitation center, and you know how a lot of people can get possessed thanks to that crap, right? Well, I'm pretty sensitive to people who are REALLY possessed, and as soon as I took it off, BAM, that feeling hit me. It was VERY unexpected, and shocked me to realize just how much my pendant was doing. Praise Yah indeed for such miracles.

Sherry said orgone stops wicked and evil beings around you. Imagine walking around a rehab clinic in the full belief that the patients were possessed by literal demons searching for people to possess or even kill. It's like being trapped in one of those live-action haunted houses where the actors don't attack you, but you feel as if they might.

The anticipation for Kelly must have been terrible. With her necklace on, though, she didn't get that feeling. The orgone protected her, and that made her feel safer and calmer. It quieted the demons and made her final mission possible. It also provided a brief bonding opportunity with her friend Marcy.

Marcy was in a bad place. She hadn't come out as gay yet to her parents and was suffering from a deep abiding depression that made Sherry's teachings attractive. Very few kids who go to religious school don't obsess over the Book of Revelations sometime between the sixth and eleventh grades, with its violent secrets wrapped in coded language for the wisest among us to prepare for the end.

Most of all, Revelations describes the only events in the Bible that haven't happened yet. Every Christian sect believes it holds the key, in one way or another, to understanding the final days. It's an appealing alternative to thinking about the future for someone whose entire life is changing at astonishing speeds.

Marcy was no different. She'd read Revelations, and as she got out in the world, she explored all sorts of esoterica. It's fun to try and divine the future, or to know for certain whether there's an afterlife and how we can assure our entry. As Marcy put it, Sherry offered her an opportunity to look away from her own life, which was demanding and spinning out of her control. She replaced it with a mystery that needed to be solved because the fate of humanity rested on it. More than that, it was something she and Kelly had in common. When they were at their loneliest and most confused, the two could work together on undermining the NWO.

By 2011, Rebekah had enrolled in Concordia College, just outside of Ann Arbor, and Kelly had moved back home. When she and Marcy drove up to visit Rebekah, Kelly tossed orgone pucks along the route. She told Marcy it was a way of protecting their path, constructing a barrier along Route 14 on the way out and back.

Kelly was making and buying enough orgone to outline every path and home in her life. She gave them to friends and to strangers, and she always wore her orgone pendant, which shows up like shined bronze in photos from the time. Crystals or metal chips run in two angular, vertical rows emphasizing the center, like primitive stitches on either side of a scar. Marcy said it was an angelic symbol.

"[Kelly] was saying that she had just realized that she was an angel and that she believed that we were all angels with missions," Marcy said of her friend. "I do remember her saying that, and that made me feel good. Why wouldn't I? Like, if I'm an angel, I'm important, I'm special."

People just want to feel important, needed, and special, and if Kelly was getting that from Sherry, all the better. What no one understood about Sherry Shriner until it was too late is what happens when that designation is taken away.

Although she almost got caught up in Sherry Shriner's cult, Marcy was fortunate enough to escape. One evening her mother came across some of the Sherry Shriner materials Marcy and Kelly had left out. Marcy's mom didn't threaten or throw a tantrum; she just told Marcy that she was really uncomfortable with her getting into something like that, and the spell broke.

Marcy didn't take it well at first. She didn't want to sever the special orgone connection she and Kelly had, but upholding the outrageous claims about reptilians and spaceships required too much intellectual and emotional energy. Paranoia can be exhausting. Marcy couldn't unsee Sherry's teachings having seen them through her mother's eyes. She and Kelly still saw one another, but Marcy was out as a potential orgone warrior.

And that's how people involved with Sherry Shriner fall away from those close to them. They're not driven out. Kelly certainly wasn't. But they understand what nonbelievers think of them. No one who is privy to the fact that reptiles run the world thinks it's a normal perspective.

As far as I could tell, many of the Shrinerites are less ashamed of their beliefs than exhausted by seeing the faces of people they care about glaze over as they realize they're talking to a conspiracy nut. On the flip side, people we think of as conspiracy nuts pity our ignorance, gullibility, and blind acceptance of the world as it appears.

* * *

Sex was a burning, confusing question for Kelly, but she found answers in the discovery that she was an Angel in the Flesh. Angels can choose a new gender whenever they're given a new earthly mission.

Kelly's LiveJournal page provides a tragic, sometimes too-intimate look into her descent: "Before I was born into flesh here on Earth, my angelic body was male," she wrote. "But I was wearied, and sick and tired of being a male, with all the roles and responsibilities that came with it, so in my heart of hearts I asked Yah not only to allow me to be born female here on Earth, but to be born extra feminine, with many luscious curves."

She was interested in boys but committed to premarital chastity. Reading her thoughts and speaking with her friends left me with the impression that Kelly was bursting with a sexual tension where curiosity knows it can't be sated. Her writing, when it left textual analysis and turned to practical everyday life in hell, could be graphic and violent, filled with torture, rape, and sex slavery. Here again, it's hard to tell whether she was influenced by Sherry or it was the other way around, but rape and torture ran strong through their descriptions of the ongoing secret war.

Sherry was much more heavy-handed on the pedophilia, but that was an earthbound political issue for her. Kelly was consumed by documenting her torments in hell, where for three years she endured a crucible wherein she witnessed and was forced to do evil. That she came through it alive confirmed her as an Angel in the Flesh. It's hard to read once you understand Kelly was not writing dark, creative fiction, but rather documenting experiences she believes she had.

Just as with orgone missions, there are irreconcilable realities; the most tenuous one is the one we all share. Kelly's friends, when they saw her writing, took it as metaphorical. She didn't discourage that view, but she didn't agree with it either. Kelly's friend

Brandon Moore, who was studying graphic design at Concordia with hopes of publishing comic books, considered Kelly's writing to be scintillating fiction.

They met in 2011, guests at Rebekah's twenty-first birthday party, and bonded over anime. Kelly's stories blew him away. They were dark and imaginative, horrible and compelling, descriptions of hell and the machinations of evil beings on earth. When she visited, she'd bring orgone to gift as they walked around campus, and Kelly would explain some of her new discoveries. As open-minded as he tried to be, Brandon just couldn't make the connection. In fact, when he finally listened to one of Sherry's shows, it baffled him that Kelly listened to such trash.

"You can believe, I guess, some pretty wild and insane theories, but if your intent is good, if you're doing it to help people, if you're not malicious in your intent, then I have no problems with it," Brandon told me. "I thought of it, like, okay, yeah, Sherry Shriner herself is like kind of a crackpot, but Kelly's not a crackpot. She's just trying to be a positive influence on the world and, I guess, open people's minds. It was weird for me, personally, because I thought, 'Kelly, you're so smart.' "

Sherry's stories and the zealots arguing about the end of the world and sharing proof about the NWO in Facebook and YouTube comments sections weren't bedtime stuff. I can confirm from my own experience that listening to hours of Sherry Shriner adds a low level of dread into your life. The pulsing introduction is madness itself, a kind of electro-dance beat featuring a hellfire preacher's tinny remonstrations against homosexuality and break dancing.

Sherry has the worst internet connection of any person making a living online. You hear the buzz before you hear her voice—a low, vibrating tone present in the background. Her voice, the voice of the goddess, is raspy from smoke, sharp and Mid-western, not as heavy as Chicago, not as southern as Kentucky.

The things she says are horrifying less for their content than for the fact that she directs them at people who trust and believe in her. The world is always ending, the government is always trying to poison you, and the church doesn't know the truth. There is no hope outside of the end of the world, which, she says, should be along any moment.

Even setting aside her metaphysical claims, you can't forget the people who are out there waiting for the end of the world or for the next revolution. A mob of terrified, hopeless people being whipped into a frenzy by a woman who isn't bound by logic and has a frothing contempt for the truth.

Listening left Brandon struggling to reconcile what an open, caring young woman had in common with such odious people. Kelly would bring groceries and take him out to eat because he was her friend and he was a broke college student. She wanted to do good things for people. Still, he could only point out to Kelly how she wasn't like the rest of the group, but it was a connection she never made.

"I'd be reading the comments and listening to the people who are like actually actively following her and be like, how can you guys live like this? You're just in constant fear," Brandon said. "This is paranoia to the utmost degree, like everyday paranoia. How can y'all function? Do y'all have jobs?"

Kelly's friends were shocked that she knew and associated with Sherry and the rest, that their inner darkness didn't drive her away. She showed an openness and a will to be good that drove her beyond what Sherry required. Kelly's Christian charity began at orgone gifting, but revolved around doing good works for God.

Kelly didn't just believe she was an angel, she also tried to act like one. That's what was so insidious about her transformation.

On the outside, she was the same: charitable and kind, interested and helpful, forthright and open. If someone's running around town doing charity and volunteering, it's hard to believe they spend their nights listening to hateful spittle dripping from some crank's mouth.

Things at home in Redford were going less well. Her brother, Nate, was worried. He knew from early on that Sherry Shriner was bad news and that her teachings had begun to corrupt his sister's mind, but he also was a big brother and had to handle it that way. In addition to chiding Kelly and challenging her on her beliefs, by 2012 Nate was an on-again, off-again troll on Sherry Shriner's Facebook page.

I'm amazed Nate wasn't more aggressive because the Sherry Shriner Facebook page is a vile place to visit. His trolling felt pointed, as if he were trying to make Sherry look foolish. It started simply enough. In August, he commented on one of Sherry's latest poisoning complaints. They poisoned her salt, she said, and announced she was looking for a salt substitute (which I guess is harder to poison).

Sherry *vaguebooked* (posting something personal or emotional, but not specific, on social media) for the same reasons lots of people do, attention and connection. But as God's Ambassador on Earth, she also needed engagement. Where some people would vaguebook, "Feeling down today," Sherry wrote about being poisoned by the government. Her followers responded as charged on her page—some offering salt alternatives while others swore off salt altogether.

Nate called them idiots. It helped kill the conversation but didn't start much of a fight. Sherry Shriner monitored the people who were allowed to comment on her page and revoked privileges often and without debate. The fact that Nate was able to comment

63

with this kind of impunity spoke to Kelly's influence as an orgone warrior.

By September 2012, the Shrinerites were losing their minds. Few doubted President Barack Obama was a reptilian Muslim, and all worked themselves into a frenzy trying to prove it before he outlawed Christianity and came for their guns. There was only one way to stop him, and that was to buy and make more orgone.

I imagine people stocking up on the stuff, placing it around their homes, maybe sitting on the couch holding some and praying. It's a funny image until you think about what's going on in their heads, how utterly terrified they must be all the time, then it's pitiable. Grown-ups holding a handful of copper- and crystal-laced resin wondering when the Muslim Inquisition will start and whether they will have the strength to fight off the hordes Obama had waiting to take over the country.

Nate was an honorably discharged soldier and a Christian who knew they were either lying or being paranoid, but he also lived with his little sister and knew about her orgone missions and fringe beliefs. The two were close, and he understood these were her friends and that this was part of her struggle with her own fears and demons. Kelly spent a lot of time in her room transcribing Sherry Shriner's absurdities and praying over her orgone for protection. Kelly had even carved angelic symbols into her bedframe.

By late fall, many people worried that the planet Niribu, also known as Planet X, was on a collision course with planet Earth. It was one of Kelly's greatest fears. She'd spoken to Nate about it. Sherry talked about Niribu all the time. It was on constant approach and only kept at bay by increased orgone production. Nate thought orgone was stupid.

"It's a war, folks! It's us against them so wake up and get busy with what Yah has given us to destroy them with and fight back with against them!" Sherry told her followers. "Our ways are not His ways, it is for us to take what He's given us and get busy with the orgone!"

This was followed by a link to her OrgoneBlasters.com page.

"I'm sure that if you got close to Obama and pointed an orgone at him that he would melt like the wicked witch," Nate commented below the link. "Riiiiiiight."

Sherry didn't rise to the bait, but it must have been a problem to let Nate continue posting unchallenged. People simply didn't contradict Sherry for long on her own page.

The final blowup looks to have been in October. Kelly had either been up all night or rose early and worked through the day. She published a 1,200-word treatise on chakras a little after 4:00 in the morning and continued writing, knocking out ten times that much before 2:00 p.m. The bulk of her manic work was a four-part commentary on Job 37, where, according to commentators, it's revealed that "the suffering of the righteous is not a token of God's enmity but of his love." That suffering is proportional to holiness is a central tenet among the Shrinerites.

With his sister sequestering herself in Sherry's service, it's no wonder Nate did what he could to undermine Sherry's influence over Kelly, but his final argument with her was personal. Sherry's rant this time included prophecy that Obama would use NATO troops to kill or round up Americans for the coming slaughter. Nate lost it.

"I mean do you people really believe that every person that works for the feds or in the military has been replaced by an alien or a robot?" he asked. "For fuck's sake, I WAS IN THE MILITARY A YEAR AGO, and trust me, they are normal people just like you and I."

He went on to argue that the US made up about 60 percent of NATO forces, but the trolls kept coming, suggesting he would follow orders if he was told to kill Americans or that he wouldn't resist or that he wouldn't help people in the ghettos of Detroit.

Nate wasn't defending his sister with the verbal assault that followed; he was defending the honorable people of the US military. It read a little like a movie speech. He talked about defending Sherry and the rest, even though they're awful and using their First Amendment rights to hurt people and lie about them. From there he reminded them how notoriously well-armed Michigan is and how, if it came to it, he and the rest of the former military people in the country would be part of a resistance.

"I would defend you and your family and your rights down to my life," he continued. "And fuck you for downplaying my morals."

Nate was relentless. He met every jibe with righteous anger and beat the entire room into submissive silence. In all of the posts I've seen on Sherry Shriner's Facebook page, I've never seen anyone shut up the entire mob the way Nate did. Along the way, Sherry had told him he was in denial of the truth, but I don't think she believed it. She had been trying to paint the US Army as just "window dressing" for Satan's forces, but Nate hit all the right notes. He was a Christian and an American and still revered his vow to serve, even though he was no longer active duty.

The last thing Sherry wanted was someone who was a former military, bona fide conservative Christian, but not a racist or a nut ball, gumming up the works. Nate was too gray for Sherry Shriner's black-and-white world. Long after the rest of them disengaged, Nate kept pounding away. After that, it was radio silence.

It's unclear whether Sherry blocked him, or if he just realized he was getting wound up over a bunch of kooks. Either way, Nate was done with Sherry Shriner—or at least that's what he must have thought.

* * *

The louder outsiders denigrate a cult, the tighter the adherents cling. It was something Sherry Shriner counted on. The orgone warriors were always under attack from Satan, and in the context of Kelly's obsession with Job 37, the approach worked. When Sherry claimed ninjas were poisoning her coffee, or that government energy rays were trained on her home, or that she was on Obama's kill list right behind Chavez, she was living the dream in her followers' eyes. Sherry was setting the bar so high that people who weren't getting tortured must have worried they weren't faithful enough.

Sherry had legitimate health problems. She was overweight, she smoked, and she had at least one heart attack. Whenever she was ill, though, it wasn't her lifestyle, it was Lucifer trying to bring her down. That was why the NWO sent spies to infiltrate Sherry's groups as a way of discrediting or undermining her until they launched a successful assassination attempt.

It bothered no one that the ancient secret cabal, which had been running the world for centuries, executing popes, kings, and presidents, hadn't been successful in offing a rural Ohio housewife because God wouldn't let them. She was like Job that way. Every failed attempt was further proof of her divine protection and served to help Sherry maintain absolute authority.

Brother Rich told a story about when they were driving around Kentucky during the Fort Knox orgone mission. The lead car, occupied by Sherry and Kelly, was beset by creatures coming out of the dark to make the car swerve. This, on top of all the spies, reptilians, and agents they saw, may have made him wonder whether they had a mole. Add to that Nate's insolence, and it wasn't a long leap to the obvious conclusion: Kelly Pingilley, who had served Sherry without recognition for the past several years, was a spy sent to undermine and possibly kill Sherry.

Especially given the attacks when Sherry and Kelly traveled together, Marianne Mulloy agreed Kelly was a super soldier and could no longer be trusted. I only know Marianne from reading her posts. She posted no photos of herself and shared few personal details. The only thing I learned about her for sure is that she was among the most vicious, relentless persecutors of people she thought had been disloyal to Sherry. She was no stranger to sending hate mail, to lying about her perceived enemies, or to threatening lower orgone warriors into silence.

She added insult to injury with such glee that in my mind she was a flying monkey tormenting the Scarecrow—as much because she liked it as because it was her mission. After consulting with Rich, whom she knew was more jealous of Kelly than anything else, she was on board. After all, even before Nate got so mouthy, Kelly had been carrying herself more like a prophet than an acolyte.

"Kelly thought she was bigger than life," Brother Rich said. "Sherry just asked me to deal with her, but I told Sherry Kelly was a fraud."

As both 2012 and the world were coming to an end, Kelly had ramped up her blog, elaborating more than ever beyond Sherry's teaching and claiming to be inspired by Yah. She had developed an internet relationship with a person who went by Butch online but whom she referred to as Phil, and they seemed to have had their own explanations about how the world was going to end and what they had to do to stop it.

The couple chatted online into the early morning. Kelly started reposting some of his work on her blog. Sherry could have been mad at Nate or jealous of Butch/Phil, but after Brother Rich and Marianne denounced Kelly, something had to be done.

Nate told me that Kelly had a falling out with Sherry. He didn't say over what, but as December 21, 2012, approached, the end of the world according to the Mayan calendar, Kelly began her lonely descent.

Meanwhile in Louisiana, a woman who went by the name MJ started making positive waves as part of Sherry Shriner's group. It would be untrue to suggest that she took Kelly's place, but it is worth noting how their lives intersected as one's star rose as the other's fell.

7

JESUS SAID THAT I HAVE TO HELP YOU NO MATTER HOW EXPENSIVE IT IS.

MJ is a pretty woman, still young-looking in her early forties, with fair skin, dark hair, and an accent that locates her squarely in the South. She describes her relationships before finding Sherry as codependent and volatile, often involving alcohol, drugs, and the kind of quest for the bottom that's almost too familiar in Christian redemption and conversion stories.

After years of struggling with her inner demons, and out of a deep desire to be able to keep and take care of her daughter, MJ went to a psychic in search of metaphysical help she couldn't get in church. She said she was sexually assaulted by demons so relentlessly that her boyfriend at the time accused her of sleeping with someone else, which she's sure she absolutely wasn't. MJ believed demons came to her at night and violated her in her sleep.

It seemed as if anywhere she went, bad things happened. Every attempt at happiness or even normalcy was thwarted by forces aligned against her. The psychic took her in and diagnosed her with possession, which came as something of a relief. She began to understand why she was having so much trouble with men, drugs, and alcohol. It was the literal demons.

"[Her psychic] said no one will believe this is happening to you. And they will want to get you definitely to stop seeing me. And we can't have that because you need to be cleansed of this," MJ told me. "And she was right. Because I tried telling someone and they were like, 'Girl okay,' you know? It was one of those things you can't tell people because they aren't going through it. They will not believe you."

After making payment arrangements, the psychic scheduled a cleansing.

"You know? You have an incredibly strong back," the psychic had told her. "No one else would be able to deal with this, but Jesus said that I have to help you no matter how expensive it is."

MJ took me through the ritual in a matter-of-fact way, the way you might talk about having a nasty mole removed from your arm, occasionally realizing you needed to be graphic, but keeping your word choice and tone as clinical as possible.

"I had to get completely undressed and stay in the bathroom for, I don't know, like an hour. And I had to put this sea salt with this oil from the Dead Sea in Jerusalem all over my body and also up inside my privates and stay there for a while. I had to, in other words, sit with that stuff on me and then shower …

"This is where the things get freaky. I went into the shower, and I cleaned off just as she said, okay? And I didn't touch my privates. I just mainly rinsed off. I wanted to keep some of that beautiful oil on me. Well, I got all showered. I was drying off and I turned around and I looked at the shower, and I couldn't believe what I was seeing. There was a pile, and it was at the bottom of the shower, it would not reach down the drain.

"It was a pile of goo, and I mean a pile. It was, like, I don't know, half a foot off the bottom of the shower, and it was opaque white, but it was clear. It was like jelly goo stuff. It was like a plasma. And in the plasma, I took a closer look. It had blood vessels all in it, and I was like, 'What kind of alien creature just came out of me?'"

Confused but feeling healed, MJ looked for an explanation about how demons could become corporeal inside a person. It took her a while to happen upon Sherry Shriner, but not long at all to get on board. After three listens to Sherry's radio show, MJ was hooked. In one of the first shows MJ heard, Sherry was speaking about demonic possession and explained that if you're the victim of a spiritual possession for long enough, it becomes physical possession. This simple connection explained everything.

MJ joined Sherry's Facebook page. She'd listen to the shows live and comment occasionally in the livestream's forum, convinced that Sherry had more answers. As it turned out, she did. According to Sherry, MJ's successful expulsion of that grim jelly meant that her "good" side, her "saved" side, was fighting back. God was calling her to a larger purpose and needed her clearheaded and pure of heart for the missions on which he, through Sherry, would send her.

MJ went back to work, was able to have her school-aged daughter with her full-time again, and spent all of her spare money and energy praying, making and gifting orgone, and sharing the truth as proclaimed by Sherry Shriner.

From the outside, it seemed a complete turnaround, and in a way, it was, but MJ still was a woman doomed to be alone. Whenever she sought companionship and started dating, something would thwart her efforts to be a little happier. Before finding Sherry, MJ's loneliness depressed her, but now that she understood the truth that her solitude validated God's favor, the consequences were easier to take. Demons possessing the people around her just to try and break her spirit only made her nicer, kinder, and more willing to help.

Sherry confirmed what MJ already knew in her heart: her endurance would be noticed and rewarded by The Most High. As 2012 wound down, MJ was well-placed to do the Lord's work as Sherry commanded.

This idea that the sickness that starts in your gut and runs through your chest isn't depression at all, but God showing his love by letting you suffer might be the worst placebo ever offered.

In addition to ticking off all the Truther boxes, including being anti-vaxxers, Shrinerites believed neither in psychiatric therapy nor in anything produced by Big Pharma. Psychological symptoms were treated by prayer and prayer alone. (In fact, when MJ was told she had to remain medicated to keep her job, she asked Sherry for special dispensation.)

Once it was clear that MJ's sickness and self-doubt were external, part of an assault by the forces of evil, MJ felt she had found her people and began her career as an orgone warrior. As MJ was feeling more and more welcomed, Kelly Pingilley was on the outs with Sherry Shriner and was quite likely expelled from the group.

* * *

I believe several things happened in the late fall and winter of 2012 that soured Sherry on Kelly. Brother Rich put the blood in the water, denouncing Kelly not long after Sherry's very public whipping by Kelly's brother, Nate. That could have been a catalyst, but only if Kelly was a legitimate threat, and Sherry had good reason to think she was.

Sherry had written about Angels in the Flesh early on, but Kelly made the idea truly magical. Her creative spirit made her own prophecy sing when compared with Sherry's drab prose. I believe that was a serious sticking point in those last weeks. Kelly claimed she was an Angel in the Flesh, but that honor was supposed to be bestowed by Sherry during one of her trips to heaven and conferred on the anointed by Beverly. You can see why Brother Rich criticized Kelly as thinking she was "bigger than life."

"She thought she was greater than Sherry, but I was too powerful for her, and I read through her bullshit," he said.

Just as with the Old Testament deity, Sherry was a jealous god. She hated when people contradicted her, but she hated not being the center of the conversation more. She accused Nate of being a narcissist in their recent tiff. Sherry wanted to talk about preparing to fight the NWO, and he turned it into a lesson on the responsibilities of being a Christian patriot.

Kelly wasn't just nicer than Sherry, she was developing her own way of thinking, improving upon the prophet's teachings with musings of her own. This couldn't have gone over well. Sherry's followers believed she was God's chosen prophet. She couldn't risk giving the impression there was another. Kelly had even published her own origin story as if she were preparing her CV for would-be followers.

Kelly put the date of her own spiritual awakening as Monday, September 28, 2009, which she would later discover was Yom Kippur, the Day of Atonement in Judaism. That was the night she learned the truth about her night terrors. Kelly claimed that for years she was kidnapped out of the bottom bunk, with her sister sleeping above, taken to hell, and tortured. She recalled waking up with bruises on her body, seeing dark beings move in the early morning gloom, and being beset by evil thoughts and impulses that didn't seem to be coming from her. Then she discovered Sherry's story and followed her teachings.

Kelly's story isn't much different from the one MJ would tell. Realizing that her tortures were the result of spiritual attacks, Kelly began to practice the art of spiritual warfare. Praying is the sidearm for the spiritual warrior, the simplest most common weapon. Warfare prayers, as they're called, are precise. You may have heard them in megachurch-type praying. The trick is to ask for something specific at a specific time in a specific way, and that way you can tell for certain whether a prayer worked.

7 Jesus said that I have to help you no matter how expensive it is.

The other key for Kelly, and a prevailing number of evangelical conspiracy enthusiasts, is not to talk about Jesus. Jesus was the made-up, early church name for Yahushua (pronounced *ya-HOO-shoo-wah*). Sherry was clear and emphatic about this. She claimed the picture of "Jesus" in churches is a demon called "Sananda," sent to fool weak-minded Christians into following Lucifer.

From her perspective, Kelly not only had been misled by the shysters or dupes of the Lutheran Church, but those same people had encouraged her to ask the wrong guy for the wrong kinds of things. Add to that the fact that Lucifer knew her to be an Angel in the Flesh, a warrior to be called upon in the coming battle, and it only made sense that she was beset by evil spirits.

Sherry's cure got Kelly cleaned out and on the right path. Knowing she was an Angel in the Flesh helped her be a better person in real life. With the possible exception of Nate, most people saw this change as crazy, but crazy for good. Christian works are something that should be endorsed, or at least not discouraged.

Her friend Britt put it best: "With her parents' divorce and finding herself as a young woman, she was pretty depressed all the time. So, I was like, 'This is making you happy, so, you know, if it's not harmful then, you know, you just do you!' " Britt's voice broke a little over our connection. "And then I have to live with that for forever."

I honestly believe Kelly never lost faith in Sherry's teachings, only in the prophet herself. Nate challenged Sherry that summer to make one prophecy that came true, but he was met with silence. He had to be. Sherry's predictions could only be accommodated to the past. The rest of Sherry's teachings were just doomsday blather, but it was blather upon which thousands of lives depended.

This isn't hyperbole. People built more than their spiritual lives to Sherry's specifications. They staked their identities on them. Belief in Sherry was an outlet for their fears and a confirmation of them. Just as Kelly did with her pendant, the orgone placebo worked wonders in the short term but depended too much on avoiding reality. Orgone can stay the blackness or terror as long as a person convinces themselves evil demons exist, but if that belief slips or changes, all the real demons (depression, anxiety, despair) rain down on them. Once it starts, reality crashes down without mercy.

* * *

In late 2012, Kelly was expelled or drifted out of Sherry's orbit. There are few clues outside of other cases where the group undertook an aggressive public shunning, but I don't suspect Kelly's was much different. The attacks tended to be both on Facebook as well as via Facebook Messenger and personal email telling the shunned that they were going to hell and that they'd been unfaithful to The Most High.

Sherry would add the final blow, claiming to never have been fooled by the now-exposed liar, playing them as a way to make Lucifer feel as if this latest plan was working before exposing them as spies and casting them out. For many of Sherry's victims, what follows is a crushing loneliness and isolation followed by a search for a new religion. But Kelly wasn't a normal victim.

Think of action movies, older war movies, say, or any clear-cut good-versus-evil story. There's a point where the hero realizes he is on his own (the brass won't listen, the chain of command is corrupt, name your trope), and that the only way to save everyone is to sacrifice himself.

Kelly looked around her and realized she was the only one who knew the truth about the coming war. Sherry said the world wasn't ending on December 21, 2012, that it would be months before the end of the world, but Kelly thought it would be sooner, and she had to help everyone get ready. Without Sherry, she couldn't make the others believe her, but the world was ending, and the devil was coming, so Kelly Pingilley had to prepare to do what she could to save mankind.

The end of the world was imminent, and Kelly was on a mission. She had a "go bag" filled with everything someone would need during the War of Armageddon: food, bottled water, and a serious supply of orgone, very much like the one Kelly had with her at all times. Marcy lived near a trailhead where hikers started and ended their treks, and Kelly enlisted her help in hiding the bag. When the war starts, she told Marcy, God might need to lead someone to it. Marcy would remember hiding the bag because it was a quintessential Kelly thing to do.

Kelly was trying to do favors for strangers while the world was ending around her. That's what made me want to tell her story. Everyone said the things you expect. Kelly was sweet, kind, and caring. What people made clear through their stories, though, was the profound sense of loss and regret. That someone so good could get so misdirected under their noses haunts them. Her friends regret not being old enough or wise enough to help, or to understand that the madness, darkness, and hopelessness Sherry Shriner spouted vibrated through Kelly, bringing her into tune with the rest of the paranoid, would-be soldiers of God.

"It is coming, you will see it," Kelly told Marcy of the apocalypse. "If it's dark for three days, do not go outside!"

Up in her room, Kelly threw herself at her blog, not telling her friends she had quit her job and stopped going to college. She wrote without sleeping, chatting with her internet boyfriend and preparing her user's guide to the end of the world. Kelly wrote thousands of words, confessing her torture, enumerating with heartbreaking detail the horrific acts that were done to her in hell, and preparing people for what might befall them in the coming days.

She wrote "The Importance of Crying," in collaboration with internet boyfriend Phil, praising the act as a release of negative energy that should be accepted and even embraced. She followed with her own commentary. It started like this:

> If you are one such person who has been programmed to NOT cry or be able to cry, even when your entire soul wants to, please know that you are not alone, and that you should not feel frustrated. There are many blocks that are put within our hearts and minds and souls to control us and further the programming, and then there are memories we suppress ourselves because they are so horrifying. Unfortunately, the only way to overcome these and find true joy and happiness is to face the memories and face the blocks and conditioning head on—and this MUST be done with Yahuah [God] and Yahushuah [Jesus].

Kelly's last entries are as disturbing as they are sad, knowing that they're spiritual biography rather than fiction. She reasoned out her beliefs sedately enough, imploring people not to go through the apocalypse alone but rather to reach out to Yahuah, who is only waiting for them to call him by his real name. At each section head, there's a prayer of some sort. Primitive and superstitious in construction, they petition The Most High to protect the reader from the words, to bring the faithful strength or kinship, and to prevent devils possessing the reader.

After preparing people for what might befall them in the coming days, Kelly changed her tenor if not her tone. Her final entry, explaining the Mark of the Beast, what it means and how to protect yourself from it, drips with paranoid empathy. She knew most readers wouldn't believe her, but held out hope that, in addition to the few that accept her warnings and advice, those who don't will recall it as the war rages on and find comfort, hope, and instruction.

Kelly made her first post a little after 4:30 p.m. Thursday, December 20, 2012, and finished writing at nearly 1:30 a.m. That evening found the four friends together at Marcy's house. Marcy remembered the date because Kelly told her she thought the world still might end that night.

As with any experience you don't know is significant until it's too late, each of the women has slightly different memories surrounding whether Kelly brought some gifts and said there were more to come, or whether she claimed to have forgotten to bring them altogether. Besides mentioning her concern that the world might still end, Kelly's behavior wasn't outrageous, and the four women spent a pleasant night with one another, remarkable only in that it was their last.

8

I'M OFF TO FULFILL MY DESTINY.

Christmas came and went for the Pingilleys. Nate remembers Kelly redistributing all of the gift cards she received, but it wasn't out of place. Kelly liked giving things to people. She liked helping the less fortunate. She was happy, cheerful even, although there still was a little tension over the end of the world, or lack thereof.

If there are any records of what she did or said in the week that followed Christmas, they were committed to her notebooks. Most of Kelly's internet records were deleted, and I was given to understand that Kelly's mother put the notebooks away. I don't blame her.

Kelly left the letters on the bed. They were her final Christmas gift to her friends, their names distinct in her loopy, still-girlish hand. She drove to town, parked, and went into the CVS. I don't imagine she shopped for long. She knew what she was there for. Kelly brought a package of Sleepinal and a bottle of acetaminophen to the counter, paid, got back in her white Buick, and drove off.

The sun was setting as Kelly headed west along Route 14. Because it was the week between Christmas and New Year's, traffic was probably light that Tuesday evening. No one knows whether Kelly knew where she was going or if she was just driving around. It had snowed, but the roads were safe under a white-gray winter sunset as another dusting loaded up for the evening. The world went purple, then that disorienting, grainy black-and-white of winter highway driving through the woods.

As she came up along the Waterloo Recreation Area, a public hunting ground and nature reserve in Jackson County, Michigan, forty minutes or so from her home, Kelly pulled into the parking area. She jotted a note on a sheet of loose-leaf from one of her journals: "Mom, Sorry for not calling. Love You."

She punctuated "Love You" with the smiley face she used in much of her writing, one that was familiar to her friends. She tucked the note in the notebooks she had packed into a white plastic shopping bag. It may have been the last thing she wrote.

She had written another goodbye earlier, but maybe she wasn't sure when it would be found:

Mom and Dad (& Nathan & Amanda/Nathan)

I'm off to fulfill my destiny. [Smiley]

I Love you all!

Sorry I can't tell you where I'm going [Side-eye smiley]

I don't know when I'll be back,

So I wanted to make sure you all knew that I loved you. [Smiley]

[In smaller print she wrote] Also sorry about the car.

[She signed it.]

~Kelly M. Pingilley [adding a heart that nearly touched the tail of the flourished cursive y.]

Again, there's the innocence, the complete openness in signing a note to your family using your full name. The more I read it, the more I wondered about how much Kelly might have seen this as a literal suicide mission.

Kelly grabbed her plastic CVS bag along with her bag of notebooks, locked the car, made her way back to Trist Road, and started walking west along the shoulder, shuffling through ankle-deep snow against the traffic. There's a break in the under-growth-choked tree line where three dilapidated posts hold up saggy barbwire indicating the easiest path through the woods and into the clearing beyond. The snow hadn't started yet, and it's easy to imagine how many stars must have been in that night sky among the gray gathering clouds. Of course, to Kelly they weren't all stars. Sherry said many of them were ships preparing for war. Planet X was up there, unseen and menacing.

I'm convinced that as Kelly took it all in and prepared herself mentally for her mission, she hoped she succeeded and could return, but was resigned to whatever path The Most High set for her.

She laid down a white plastic bag that she brought with her. In it were her notebooks, where she drafted and elaborated upon the stories that made it onto her blog. Notebooks were important to Kelly. Their abandonment is, for me, one of the strongest pieces of evidence that Kelly hoped she'd return.

As her friends, family, and people like me tried to get a handle on Kelly's mission that night, there emerged a cacophony of pointless conjecture. The only harmony is the point that Kelly believed she was going to join God in the war. Some people said Kelly believed she had the key to hell and had to return it to God before the war started. Others say she was going to meet her internet boyfriend Phil, or some combination of the two. From this distance, though, we weren't very different than the Shrinerites, distracted from the hard truth of the world by mystical speculation.

Kelly walked for a short while, spread out her blanket, sat down, and made herself comfortable. Before too long, it started to snow.

9

MURDERED BY A NATO DEATH SQUAD.

The two boys weren't up exceptionally early for winter break, but they did get a jump on the cold, clear day. Whether they crossed Trist Road near the riding stables bordering Waterloo Recreation Area because they saw footprints in the snow or if they happened upon them while exploring was secondary to the discovery.

Few people sauntered along the country road in the harsh Michigan winter. There were few houses, and this being late morning, it was unlikely that a hunter still was about. When the tracks left the side of the road through the brush to the clearing, the boys followed, taking care as they negotiated the small slope.

I have never ventured into a ravine or stand of trees without a voice in my head saying, "I wonder if I'm going to find a body." When I see a weird outcropping or a split-open trash bag, there's both dread and adrenaline as well as the overwhelming sense of relief tinged by minor embarrassment when my foolishness reveals itself. That is not what happened to these kids.

As they made their way into the clearing, they saw her. It could have been the purple tank top that first caught their eyes, then the jeans and the boots, and, finally, the stillness. This was a dead body. They moved closer, coming within thirty feet of the small figure. At that distance, there was no doubt. They called out anyway, as we all imagine we would have, hoping we were wrong but knowing we weren't.

No response and still no movement. Adventurers or no, they weren't going a step closer. They ran to tell their parents, who confirmed their find and kept their distance while they waited for the police.

Deputy Nicholas A. Warner pulled up to the cluster of people along the side of Trist Road. The assembled hadn't gotten too close, but they had told the dispatcher the body appeared to be that of a thirteen-year-old girl. As he approached, Warner was careful to notice one set of footprints leading up to the body, but none leading away in any direction. It was a cold, bright Michigan morning. A day made for sledding. A blue-sky day where the temperature is life-affirming, if not particularly pleasant. A too-well-lit and hopeful backdrop for the day that was about to unfold.

Police cars started showing up out on the highway, spilling out sheriffs to canvass and collect evidence. Detective Sergeant Timothy Schlundt made his way through the trees and brush to where, fifty yards further on, the incident scene waited. Warner brought him up to date. No one had been near the body before Warner when he confirmed she was dead and had been for hours. He also noted a white Buick had been left overnight in the Department of Natural Resources lot a few hundred yards east on Trist Road. He ran the plate and got back a driver's license photo.

The woman lying in the snow was Kelly Marie Pingilley.

Kelly looked to have sat down facing more or less the direction from which she'd come, east into where the sun would rise. Her green winter coat and yellow hooded sweatshirt had been set aside as had what the police described as a multicolored blanket. Her passport, license, and the receipt and change from her CVS trip were in her coat pocket. An open bottle of Ice Mountain water and a clear Ziplock bag were in the snow beside her. The bag had, among other things, her keys, three flashlights, a bottle of acetaminophen, and blister packs from the thirty-two Sleepinals.

Schlundt tugged a bit on the blanket, shuffling off the new snow to reveal two broken mechanical pencils, a pair of broken glasses, and what they described as "a Cutco medical-grade scalpel."

Cutco is only mentioned once in the reports; most of the rest of the accounts just say scalpel. As far as I've been able to tell, the company doesn't make a medical-grade scalpel. They make knives that I'm sure could be taken for scalpels. It would be a forgettable inconsistency except for Kelly's connection to Rebekah, and the time they spent learning to be single young women selling Cutco knives in Adrian, before Kelly's mind grew dark while her demeanor lightened. A time when Kelly was alive and just getting a handle on the idea of going back and forth between Earth, heaven, and hell. A time when she only had one reality and one dimension to worry about.

I obsess over that as do a few of the people I've spoken with about it. I believe that Kelly thought she was coming back, or at least hoped that she might. She had been to hell many times and had returned. She recalled being a male angel and understood that Angels in the Flesh have to take on multiple difficult missions.

Sherry talked about visiting with Yah and returning as herself. Lots of people had, and Kelly was at least as faithful to The Most High. Then there was the farewell note to her family, "Sorry about the car." You want to ask whether she was sorry that the car was abandoned, or that she planned to make her trip to heaven leaving her human shell in the Buick.

The horror tale that I tell myself goes something like that. Kelly driving aimlessly, knife in her ever-present go-bag, decides to pick up pills instead. If she had a destination in mind at the time, only Kelly knows. Her friends didn't have any insight as to why she would have chosen to head out to the country.

Once she was settled on the blanket, she was ready to do God's will. The police would discover a small "abrasion at the base of her neck near the jugular notch." Maybe the knife hurt more than she thought it would, or maybe she didn't want to chance not coming back with a new body. Worse, maybe it was a flash of doubt. Maybe Kelly had a glimmer that if she was mistaken, she would be committing suicide. Rather than take that chance, she may have decided to make an offering, putting herself in a position of spiritual availability. If she took the pills and God didn't need her as desperately as she imagined, he could deliver her, and she would wake up cold and embarrassed someplace.

It might seem pointless to speculate on her goals or state of mind, but we want to understand Kelly's cryptic goodbye. We want to know how she could have been, or could have become, that unhinged without arousing more suspicion. My speculation is driven by an affinity for Kelly, a genuine goodwill that came from reading her blog and speaking with her friends. Each and all of them were crippled by regret for not having noticed.

"She mentioned the end of the world and a World War III happening, and that she didn't think she would be around to see it," Britt said. "And I was like, 'Where are we going? Because if you're moving, I'm moving with you.' And she was like, 'I just don't know yet.' And now, years later. I was clearly young and dumb and didn't know what she had meant at the time."

When the police told Kelly's father what had happened, Nate was there as well. When I asked him about it, he struggled with the wording. The best he could do, even seven years after the fact, was to say he was shocked but not surprised. He worked to qualify that statement, worried it might sound callous, but I think I know exactly what he meant.

Imagine a well-executed movie twist where the more you think about it, the more sense it makes, even though you couldn't have seen it coming in a million years. Baffling on its own, the more you think about the story, the more inevitable it seems. But Kelly's suicide wasn't a movie, and all of Kelly's friends continue to struggle with the parts of the story they wish they could have changed.

* * *

Sherry Shriner was not grief-stricken when she heard about Kelly's death. She was in her glory. This was a young woman she had traveled and laughed with, who had transcribed her drivel and hung on her every word. A young woman Sherry recently had denounced as a traitor, sentenced to be hounded from the pack like a sick animal with the meaner, more ferocious curs snapping at her heels until she was well away and alone, forced to take on Satan's army by herself.

Sherry concocted a dish of fetid meat and honey and threw it to the assembled. Officially, Kelly died of either a sleeping pill overdose, hypothermia, or a combination of the two. Sherry got word December 30, 2012, sometime after midnight and posted on her Facebook page that Kelly was dead, but in her own Sherry way.

"What happened to Kelly Pingilley?" she wrote. "I just got a message she 'committed suicide' … there's no way she'd do that … I'm in total shock."

She added that she'd gotten some hate mail telling her Kelly killed herself. I like to think the message came from Nate, who told me he wrote to Sherry to call her a piece of shit for what she did to his sister, but anyone who knew Kelly was involved with Sherry could have sent it. She waited a beat for her swarm to notice the post, so she could begin her disinformation. After all, it was nearly 2:00 a.m. Then Sherry made the first comment under her post: "And of course it will pass as just a suicide."

Sherry had set the top and watched it spin. After a short time, people were talking about investigating to find out how Kelly "really" died. Brother Rich and Beverly Nelson offered their prayers and hopeful commentary on the thread. It took Sherry fewer than twelve hours to confirm what really happened.

Kelly Pingilley had been driving along minding her own business when she was ambushed by a NATO hit squad, the same one that had been traveling internationally taking out people who belonged to Yah. They dragged her from her car screaming and out into the woods where they murdered her and made it look like a suicide.

This is where we get our first good glimpse into the troll culture that Sherry Shriner created, encouraged, and fed. This is where the vitriol and backbiting take center stage and give a little insight into what the Shrinerites do to people who cross them.

The holidays had come and gone, and Kelly's funeral was set for Sunday, January 6, 2013. It's a tragedy too many of us experience, that first death after high school when we're forced to contend with the fact that strangers aren't the only people who die young. After the funeral, Kelly's friends made their way to Marcy's to have a drink and a cry, play some board games, and tell stories about their friend. Britt checked her phone, as much out of habit as anything else, and saw there was a message from Kelly. It said she was still alive. Faking her own death had been easy.

"Somebody told me that they had read her journals, and I was in them, and some stuff had happened in the journals, but they were like her dreams, so they were also confusing to her, and then they told me that it was my fault," Britt said. "I was young, so I believed them, but after so many years, you know, even with therapy, it's still hard."

There also was a post on Kelly's Facebook page claiming that she had faked her death. It was something people would talk about for years. Mike Hall, an avid Shrinerite, remembers it clearly.

"The day after she was killed, I was on her Facebook page, and there was a post on her fucking page by her," he said. "Moments like that just give me more confirmation that the whole Sherry Shriner ministry was legit. Like, holy fuck, one of her fuckin' followers has been taken out by the fucking CIA? Now they're taking over her Facebook and fucking making these comments?"

Sherry gave them Kelly's death as proof of her divinity, and they ate it all up. It fed Mike's paranoia and made him a more devoted follower than he already had been.

"I'm a part of something that's, it's like this secret war going on in the world," he said. "I truly believe that there is some secret fucking war going on in the world that the majority are not aware of, a spiritual war."

Nate saw the post about Kelly being killed by NATO, and he was absolutely furious. He showed Brandon Moore, who was flabbergasted by this point. They took their shots, but there was no point in feeding trolls this vicious.

"At the end of the day I knew like, what could I really do?" Brandon said. "Besides block her and try my best to like, you know, ignore her and know that the people who really knew Kelly, well—"

He was stuck, less unsure what to say next as exhausted by contemplating a world where such nonsense needed to be given voice.

"No one who really knew and loved Kelly would try to profit," he said. "She was the only one trying to use it to rally troops, so to speak."

"Rally the troops" is an understatement. Sherry was getting heat. She did interviews with newspapers and blogs, and then set her warriors on the comments sections to defend her as needed and post links to her articles and shows. She wrote a remembrance post on her page that focused as much on the psy-op the government was running to discredit Sherry as it did on Kelly. It was the first draft in an evolution of the myth about Kelly's death that would endure and evolve over the years.

For all her memorial's flowery language, by the time Sherry broadcast her first show after Kelly's death, it was no longer a topic upon which she dwelt. I don't know how far in advance Sherry planned her shows. They sound as if she was making them up as she went along. Whether by accident or design, though, the show played like Sherry Shriner 101, as if she were expecting a new crowd.

Without specific mention of her former protege, Sherry launched into the "hows" and "whys" of orgone, threw in some tripe about a recently crashed spaceship, and moved along to talk about the First-Fruits and the Warrior Elect. These were Kelly's favorite topics and the words from which she took her blog title. They're esoteric references to the broader concept of Angel in the Flesh, but if anyone was searching the internet for content related to Kelly's death using these keywords, they would find their way to Sherry Shriner. And if anyone tuned in to see what Sherry was all about, they'd get a substantial primer. Besides, her hordes were already working on the NATO myth for her.

* * *

A young man typed furiously at his computer, sharing and commenting. He had just lifted the post about Kelly's murder and abduction from Sherry's Facebook page and was working on a snazzier headline. He came up with this (rendered as I found it):

Kelly Pingilley Was Murdered By A "NATO Death Squad / Tyrannical Government"

They are assassinating people all over the world! They are trying to take us out one by one, as quiet as they can. If they can they will try to make your death look like a suicide. Do what you got to do to keep yourself safe! If you are one of gods people/fighting to get the truth out etc … They're Coming For You!

Everyone ask God/Yahua to END the life's of all those who are involved with the "NATO death squad's."

His is way more eye-catching than Sherry's boring "Remembering Kelly Pingilley" headline. It was time to take the fight to the New World Order. Martial law, economic collapse, and the return of the anti-Christ were just beyond the horizon, and he would be ready.

Sitting in his parents' home in North Arlington, New Jersey, Steven Mineo hit "Post."

10

THIS IS INSANITY! WHAT ARE YOU DOING?

No matter what awful things Shrinerites do or say, people only want to talk about the crazy beliefs. Kelly being crazy is why she died. To admit more is to open an uncomfortable conversation about religious belief and mental health. Dismissing an entire religious community as crackpots excuses the ways mean and corrupt conspiracy theorists mine people's fears. It disregards the way depression and loneliness affect so many people and, I think, gives us an excuse to believe things in our world are better than they are.

Four years later, when he was the one suffering Sherry Shriner's expulsion, Steven Mineo would see Kelly's death in a very different light. For now, he was as smitten as the rest of them to be in the presence of someone so targeted by the New World Order. He was proud to serve Sherry Shriner and be part of her horde.

Steven Mineo was a victim of a slow, methodical alienation that he initiated and participated in. He had a family who loved him and a girlfriend who, at the very least, was infatuated with him. As with Kelly, Steven was portrayed as having taken leave of his senses.

Thinking about the last few months of his life, I struggle to keep clear of that narrative, filled with mystical worlds and secret cabals, fascinating and enticing as it is. This isn't a story about crazy people; it's a story about vulnerable people being driven to the limit.

Having soaked up all the attention she was able from Kelly's death, Sherry Shriner set her sights on a new catastrophe: preventing the planned Super Bowl bombing. Before she broadcast her January 7, 2013, radio show, Sherry talked up the big game on Facebook, hinting that the codes had something to say about it.

In her show, she made it clear. The last attack on the Super Bowl had been five or so years before, when the aliens planned on blowing up Candlestick Park. This year they planned on blowing up the Superdome in New Orleans, and she was going to need some dedicated orgone warriors to go out and stop it. The San Francisco 49ers had been in both the Candlestick Park and the Superdome Super Bowls, and Sherry wondered at the significance. Eventually it hit her. Why blow up the 49ers? Because 4+9=13 and 13 is an Illuminati number.

It took me almost no time to confirm that the 49ers never played in the Super Bowl at Candlestick Park. No one has. The NFL never had the game there. In fact, when Sherry spoke about the failed bombing attempt, the 49ers hadn't even hosted an NFC championship (which a non-fan might conflate with a Super Bowl) for eighteen years.

I'm not just being pedantic here, I'm demonstrating the kinds of lies Sherry tells without consequence. Some prophets, the most successful ones, keep their lies to the metaphysical: "God told me this, God told me that." Sherry was beyond these trivialities.

Over more than a decade of radio shows, broadcasting as many as three times a week, Sherry provided (and her adorers accepted) an alternate version of reality. Ignoring facts is their default setting. It isn't just limited to crazy beliefs. Devotion to an alternate reality is nurtured in Sherry's universe and then applied to everyday life.

Sherry and her crew didn't just say that the Sandy Hook school shootings were a psy-op. They believed it. Many people did, and still do, but not because they're crazy. These things happen in their reality. Orgone warriors get dragged out of bed and murdered. They had just seen as much. There is a secret war raging, and orgone was the only useful weapon. It can't be overstated: Sherry's job, her literal way of making a living, was convincing people to make and buy orgone while supporting her prophecy-making business. It was all and everything she did.

Referencing the Sandy Hook shootings, Sherry said the New World Order had kicked off a massive psy-op as a counter strike. It may be the closest she had yet come to acknowledging Kelly Pingilley on her radio show:

> They want retaliation, and so, yeah, I do expect the war to be on. The war's gonna be on against me, and I just sit here and yawn and go out to the garage and make orgone. I'm not real worried about it. But what does anger me is their PSYOPS because they effect people. If they wanna come against me, that's fine, but they tend to go after the innocents. And they've got this huge PSYOP thing going against me. They couldn't find ways to make the orgone look bad because orgone is a positive, healing life-energy force, and there's nothing bad about it. It doesn't do anything bad. It can heal you. It can make you feel better. It stops night terrors. It stops wicked and evil beings around you.

The never-ending pitch for orgone wasn't an accident. Orgone was the perfect placebo. I think of Kelly going from panicked to calm when she put her orgone pendant on for protection from demons at work. If you believe in one of Sherry's miracles, you believe in them all. For Kelly, it was her pendant. For MJ, the woman in Louisiana whose demons had been exorcized as jelly, it would be the Super Bowl.

* * *

Listening to Sherry and reading the posts on Facebook, MJ learned there might not be enough orgone planted to protect the

Superdome. New Orleans didn't have any active orgone warriors (thus, Hurricane Katrina), and things looked bleak. Like the tentative student in the back raising her hand, volunteering for something no one, including her, believes she's equal to, MJ offered to take the lead.

She didn't have enough money to buy more orgone just then, but if Sherry would extend her some credit, MJ would drive to New Orleans and orgone the Superdome. She told me the story with wonder and a little ecstasy. Sherry would send the orgone, and they could worry about who would pay for it later on. This was an emergency after all, and no time to quibble over pennies. That was another regular theme in Sherry's sermons. People who don't want to, or can't go out and gift orgone, can donate to help wage the orgone war. Sherry passed the hat for the New Orleans mission.

MJ recruited a friend, and the pair headed to New Orleans, orgoned to the hilt. It was only a couple hours, a day trip, and when they arrived, they spread orgone wherever they could. Near the stadium as well as in the surrounding parking lots and entrances. New Orleans was covered. The Super Bowl kicked off without a hitch.

Then, two minutes into the second half (which started three minutes late because of a Beyoncé overrun), the lights went out. There was a moment, I'm sure, where every Shrinerite watching braced for the shock wave, held their breath to see the cameras blow out, stifling the screams of pain from the assembled, but the moment passed. It was just a blackout.

The official word was the system installed to prevent blackouts malfunctioned and caused one, but that's exactly what you would expect them to say. The Shrinerites knew better. MJ had saved tens of thousands of lives and billions of dollars in damage. She truly was blessed, and the Shrinerites celebrated.

It looked like 2013 was going to be a good year for MJ. She was starting to get a little notoriety in the group after proving her chops as a field asset. There was even a guy who was interested. MJ had taken another crack at dating. She found a Christian man, and they hit it off, but they got to that point, that terrible, horrible place, where she introduced him to Sherry Shriner via her radio show.

"He called her a crackpot and said, 'This is insanity! What are you doing?'" she told me. "And that was one of the things that let me know we weren't compatible."

Not loving and following Sherry was a romantic relationship deal-breaker. It was a compatibility litmus test man after man in MJ's life was doomed to fail.

Not long after saving the Superdome, MJ received a call from Sherry's close advisor and alleged major donor Beverly Nelson. She was also an Angel in the Flesh who told MJ she was the royal seamstress in heaven, making robes for God and his entourage. Beverly also bestowed Angel in the Flesh status on people based on her conferences with Sherry. When Sherry saw one of her followers during her many trips to heaven, she would tell Beverly, who would then confer the honor on the grateful acolyte.

MJ's sister had died of a terrible disease years before, but MJ always suspected that, had her sister lived, she would have been an Angel in the Flesh. She had asked as much of Sherry, and whether the prophet had seen her sister in heaven, but never received an answer. MJ felt it, though, the certainty her sister had interceded on her behalf to expel the demon manifesting inside her. Beverly said Sherry had spoken to Father and told her that MJ was indeed an Angel in the Flesh. She was still as happy to recount the information years later, I think, as she was the first time she heard it.

* * *

If MJ was going to find a man in her life, he would have to understand they were first-responders in the war against evil. Someone who also was an Angel in the Flesh. Someone who already was in Sherry's world.

Steven Mineo was one likely candidate. Steven and another orgone warrior (MJ said she couldn't remember who) messaged her and arranged a call. She and Steven clicked straight off, but MJ didn't get her hopes up. He lived in New Jersey at the time, and she in Louisiana. Neither was interested in moving or cultivating a long-distance relationship, so there could be nothing but friendship and affinity between them. He was a big fan of her work at the Super Bowl. In fact, when the game came to New Jersey's MetLife Stadium the next year, Steven orchestrated his own orgone mission to defend it.

MJ was a fan of Steven's videos, rough-cut affairs featuring prepper how-tos, reposts of footage claiming proof of martial law in America, and, of course, myths supporting Sherry Shriner. Steven considered himself a guerrilla journalist fighting the NWO. His website, Alternative News (truthseekerblog.blogspot. com), was a running commentary on news reports. The videos are gone, but the titles remain. They're called things like, "Real Life Shapeshifters Exposed" and "Christmas Is a Pagan Holiday."

Sherry appreciated Steven's efforts on YouTube, but his true value was as an apostle and evangelist. At the time, he was in his late twenties, lived with his parents, and didn't have a job to speak of. Steven could devote a lot of energy to promoting Sherry. From his perspective, he was doing God's work, so he didn't need a job. He had a mission.

As he searched the internet for proof of NWO malfeasance, Steven would use his encyclopedic knowledge of Sherry's teachings to help spread her word. For instance, if he found a video about giants walking among us, Steven would comment on its truth and leave a link to Sherry's best show or article on giants. Working from a list of Sherry-provided websites, forums, and YouTube pages, Steven lurked wherever potential new recruits went for news.

I think Steven's efforts might have been the single most useful driver for Sherry besides her radio show. As few as a thousand motivated people could generate a million hits if they were strategic enough in sharing and posting Sherry's links. That was one of Steven's dreams. He wanted to produce a viral video spreading the truth about Sherry's war with Lucifer and the NWO and the coming of martial law and economic collapse—anything that gave him a sign he was on the right path.

According to his mother, Donna Mineo, the 9/11 attacks shook Steven to his core. He grew up in North Arlington, not far from where I did in New Jersey, and although I had moved away long before the attacks, every time I go home, I get a little reminder about how 9/11 still weighs on people who live within sight of the new New York City skyline. It's not the depression or shock so much as the shaken confidence that I notice. The friendliness that I used to hear in good-natured aggression between strangers is dampened or missing.

I think it's appropriate that they called the Twin Towers site Ground Zero because it radiated the genuine outrage and fear that mutated into paranoia as it rattled through the country. For a place that was always happy to mock our Southern brethren for their backward ways, a lot of Confederate flags started popping up in New Jersey once the "American flag on the car" fad burned off in 2003 or so. The attacks rattled people's belief in both secular and divine authority, and neither institution did much to try to win that confidence back.

Lots of people fled the area. Steven wanted to be one of them, but he didn't have a job, a skill, or even a driver's license.

He fancied himself a survivalist, but he was a survivalist who depended on rides from friends or public transportation. Sherry praised the Poconos, a mountain resort in Pennsylvania, ninety minutes or so from New York City, where she sometimes vacationed. Where cities were corrupt NWO strongholds, rural areas offered more protection and fewer immediate threats. Sherry told Steven it would be the perfect place to hole up and make a stand as the war neared.

Steven wasn't so much unemployed as disinterested in working for someone else. He participated in a free e-book MLM, selling a code to download hundreds of e-books, and strung together a few dollars here and there salvaging and repairing electronics for resale on eBay. The salvage operation turned out to be an extension of something Steven had done for much of his life.

Donna told me she bought him a starter computer when he was little, six or so years old, which he proceeded to take apart, poke around in, and rebuild. That was the start of it. The family developed a side-hustle with Steven and his brother, Charles, salvaging everything electronic. Donna would grab broken items at flea markets or estate sales, and the boys would put them in working order.

She didn't say whether she bought it or Steven fixed it, but Steven came into possession of a video camera and found his vocation. He started making movies featuring his toys and his guinea pig, Red Eye.

Steven obsessed over the idea of being in the military, but his father, Steven Sr., who had served with the 82nd Airborne, discouraged his sons. Steven would have been about seventeen when the war in Iraq kicked off, and between the shock of the attacks and his father's stance on enlisting, Steven gave up on the idea of traditional military service.

When he stumbled across Sherry Shriner while researching the truth about 9/11, probably around 2010 or so, Steven saw that not all warriors are members of the military. Why be saddled with superiors and long marches? As an orgone warrior, he could fight the real enemy, here on his home soil where it was doing the most harm. Steven wanted to be accepted and looked up to. He wanted to go on missions that mattered, that helped derail the alien invasions, and that supported the orgone war.

Steven also was ready to find a girlfriend. Like MJ, he would have preferred a fellow Shrinerite. In fact, it is as likely as not that he and his friend called MJ as they were going through Sherry's Facebook followers looking for attractive, available partners. Plenty of religious people meet potential mates in church, but this church was virtual. Few people used their real names or photos. Time was Steven's ally, though. After all, he was a young man with the rest of his life ahead of him.

11

I FOUND A PURPOSE IN MY LIFE.

Sherry was catching fire. If the election of the first Black president had heated up interest about the New World Order and the end of the world, Barack Obama's re-election sent the ultra-conservative over the edge.

In 2015, once it became clear that the "libtards" were going to try and replace a Black guy with a woman in the following year's election, Sherry had carte blanche for making Obama-themed doomsday prophesies and tens of thousands of terrified pairs of ears dying to hear them. It was time for Sherry to write another book.

Interview with the Devil: My Conversation with Lucifer was to be Sherry's gospel, an account of the time Father took Sherry to heaven to interrogate the devil, whom he had imprisoned and compelled to answer truthfully. It was written interview-style, but less like a Q&A and more like a Socratic dialogue. I bought it. It was too bad to be funny. I was sick with embarrassment after every line, the way you might feel during an earnest recital where your heart breaks a little over the distance between aspiration and talent. It was the closest I ever came to pitying her.

Sherry's big reveals in *Interview with the Devil* included confirmation about the existence of Angels in the Flesh and an entirely new Christian pantheon. Jesus, as it turned out, had a sister. Sherry pretended not to be surprised, but feigned satisfaction at having her divinity confirmed. According to Sherry's followers, there's a passage where she recalls playing with Baby Jesus and Baby Lucifer before time, before the rebellion and the Fall, back when they were just three eternal siblings doing whatever it is baby angels do.

I honestly couldn't get that far in the book. Remember, though, the Bible isn't much of an end-to-end read either. *Interview with the Devil* wasn't crafted as literature. It was holy writ, a source that could be cited without worrying about inherent contradictions.

More than a decade had passed since the millennium, and God hadn't shown his face. Unemployment, underemployment, and a plummeting standard of living pressured people into looking for hope from above. The assault on the family and traditional values, "natural" disasters that drove people from their homes, Muslims, and the glitzy promises of secular life all became factors as people fled the churches they believed had failed them.

When there still was silence from the heavens after 2012, people started to wonder whether the traditional churches even had anything to offer them. For people who had only recently come to learn they'd been betrayed by the mainstream media, concluding that mainstream religion was corrupt to the core may have been the final straw. Sherry and people like her—con artists, professional paranoids, and polemicists—were in the driver's seat, and the meter was running.

Orgone sales were booming, especially as she got red hot in 2016, but Sherry walked a difficult line. Her support always had been based on her ability to convince and cajole, to borrow, repurpose, or flat-out steal rising ephemeral ideas and claim them as her own. Tearing down Barack Obama was easy and expected, as was going after Bill and Hillary Clinton, but Sherry's fight with the NWO was older and even more bitter than that. She'd written about the Bush dynasty and their alien plan. She'd denounced their participation in satanic rites and had republished photos that proved they were shapeshifters and reptilians.

Donald Trump's candidacy and then his presidency should have been a traditional and easy target, but her attacks on him didn't play as well as she expected. Sherry learned well before many of her liberal detractors that Trump was bullet-proof among her congregation and ones like it. What Hillary Clinton called deplorables were in fact heartbroken, small-minded people watching in terror as their beliefs and culture crumbled around them. Sherry and her constituents were among the first to recognize this and soften their anti-government position when it came to Trump.

After having decried him as a clone and an alien early on, Sherry adjusted Trump's position to "placeholder" as opposed to reptilian overlord or anti-Christ. He was the first American president in generations to not be on the New World Order payroll. In fact, Sherry provided occasional commentary on how the New World Order was thwarting Trump in his attempt to enact NESARA, the economic reset. Over time, all the spiritual sharks devolved into remoras as anti-Trump prophesies died on the vine without bearing cash or clicks.

As Sherry made her big push for the May 2015 release of her book, Brother Rich began worrying she was losing sight of the mission, that it was more about her and less about God. He approached her as a friend and told her his genuine concerns. By then, Sherry had started going by the name of Queen Shazurazy after having her angel name revealed to her, and I'm sure it was getting to be a little much. Sherry wouldn't change her ways, wouldn't do what God wanted her to do, so Brother Rich broke off all connection.

That's a fair account of his version of it, anyway. Sherry's version is a little different. According to her, Richard Brown was an FBI spy all along.

* * *

So much about the Richard Brown betrayal story is incoherent and contradictory that even a thumbnail sketch is going to have problems, but according to one of Sherry's versions, Richard Brown was a fallen angel, a guard at one of heaven's gates who joined Lucifer's rebellion.

Sometime around the turn of the century (Sherry is fuzzy on the date), he was arrested for drugs and cut a deal with the FBI to infiltrate and inform on Sherry Shriner and her followers. Sherry was well aware of this from the beginning. She liked keeping her enemies close. Then, Richard tried to poison her at an Arby's. He followed that little stunt by skipping the New York trip and telling Lucifer's people where to find them. Fortunately, God had cloaked Sherry and showed her the agents making their plans in front of her hotel, and the mission wasn't compromised.

Then, at some point, God had enough. He ripped Richard Brown's soul from his body and cast it into hell. Richard was replaced by a clone that turned out to be faulty and fell from a ladder and died. After that, Richard, a Black guy, was replaced by a White Richard Brown on Facebook. At that point, David, Richard's FBI handler, also was captured and disappeared by God. It's a lot to try and keep straight, which is part of the problem with making sense of Sherry's stories.

Shocked at having been pronounced dead and in hell, Brother Rich tried to counter the story. He made a couple of videos claiming that Sherry Shriner wasn't delivering God's real message, and that, in her hubris, Sherry had abandoned serving The Most High and delved into paganism.

As well-loved as Brother Rich had been only hours before her denunciation, afterward he was reviled. He got hate mail from friends, was deleted from some of his favorite Facebook groups, and eventually just faded into obscurity, left on his own to serve God in the way he saw fit.

After the release of *Interview with the Devil*, the Shrinerites started referring to Lucifer as Lucy. Higher-ranking people like Sherry, Beverly, and Marianne started referring to God as Dad as well, which is almost too precious to bear. Of the two accounts of their falling out, I tend to think Richard's is closer to the truth. First, he's still alive, which Sherry disputes, but, second, I imagine no matter how crackpotted your approach to the divine may be, when someone claims she is Jesus's sister and, on that evidence, starts referring to God as Dad, you start to wonder whether they're making some of this stuff up.

Mike Hall, for one, wasn't at all surprised to hear Brother Rich was in fact a spy who was cast into hell. Richard was always posting warrior prayers and acting as if he were the final word on scripture. Mike and he got into it more than a few times online. It made perfect sense to Mike that a guy who attacked him so thoroughly would be a satanic agent; he knew this "piece of shit" was a traitor all along and was glad his soul was burning in hell.

Mike was twenty-nine years old and ecclesiastically adrift when he came to Sherry Shriner's ministry. He knew God must have a plan for him and searched until it was revealed. He started with alt-right radio personality Alex Jones, where he learned about the Illuminati and the NWO. From there he found his way into darker recesses of David Icke, a reptilian conspiracy authority, whose message resonated. As a Christian who wanted to look into aliens and the NWO but needed a biblical reason, Mike was Sherry's ideal target audience.

Mike lived a quiet life somewhere in Canada, not far from Chicago. It occurred to me that by the time Brother Rich was cast out, Mike was approaching his late thirties and had been following Sherry for almost a decade. He seemed to have a good marriage, or at least not one worth complaining about. He had a couple of young kids who watched TV, had bedtime, bath time, and soccer practice. He had neighbors and a house. With the exception of the orgone pendants everyone in his family wore, there was nothing obvious about their religious bent. People in his life didn't know he worried about whether they were reptilians or spies. He was as real and true a believer as they come.

"I found a purpose in my life," Mike said. "I found I was meant to be an orgone warrior. I was so drawn to that."

As Mike committed more time and money to Sherry Shriner and her orgone crusade, members of his family worried he was going too far. He cut them off. Anyone who would attack his devotion to Sherry and orgone was doing it under demonic possession, or out of antipathy for the truth. He had to protect his wife and kids from anti-Sherry influence.

Without too many ties outside the Shrinerites, Mike was able to get an impressive amount of orgone made and gifted. So much so that Beverly called him after a few years of service to let him know he was an Angel in the Flesh. So committed was Mike that Sherry would refer Canadian orgone requests to him.

As early as 2011, Mike was making and shipping orgone all over Canada and even into the US. He doesn't appear to have sold it, though he made it at his own expense, shipped it at his own expense, and still sent thousands of dollars to Sherry for her to continue the mission.

"I felt so important. I felt loved. I felt I was doing something right for Yah," he said. "It was just awesome. I found my place in this world, and it felt good. And then for this fucking bullshit to go down, are you fucking kidding me?"

It's not clear whether it was on the 2012 trip with Kelly or another New York City orgone mission (the information didn't come to light until the summer of 2016), but while in New York with Sherry, Marianne said she saw Kristy Hall, Mike's wife, shape-shift on a busy city street as she followed the orgone warriors with an aim of undermining their mission.

It was a charge both Mike and Kristy denied, claiming they hadn't left Canada.

A few of the Shrinerites tried to suggest that maybe Marianne was mistaken, and it wasn't Mike's wife who shapeshifted, but Sherry shut them down, asking why they would put themselves on the line for reptilians and traitors. Endorsing the accusation opened the floodgates, and Mike, like Richard before him, got a good look at how vicious his former orgone warrior comrades could be. He had cut off all of his non-Shrinerite friends and family, and now had been cut off by Sherry and all his former friends.

"We were in a chat room called Sherry's Orgone Warriors," Steven Mineo would tell Mike later. "And she was like, 'Anybody have anything to say on this?' and they all just attacked like a pack of rabid dogs."

Before Sherry created the Mike Hall myth, a public commenter asked her if Mike was FBI. She said he wasn't, only that he had disrespected her. I think the disrespect she referred to is an incident where a stranger Facebook-messaged Mike asking for his address, and Mike dismissed him, only to later discover Sherry referred them. It calls to mind a mob movie where someone gets whacked for accidentally disrespecting the boss's cousin, but Mike never connected the disagreement to his ouster. He told the story as a way of explaining that he only ever had one negative encounter with Sherry, not as a way of explaining his expulsion. As far as Mike ever knew, he was dismissed for being married to a reptilian.

By November 2016, everything normal about this falling out had been brushed aside for the final draft, featuring Mike as a CIA agent and his wife as a reptilian shapeshifter.

"It was really hard," Mike said. "You make these friends that you even consider family and you have a love for them, and the next thing you know they're turning their back on you and calling you the most hideous things."

It's the viciousness that always gets me. Not happy with defaming a loyal orgone warrior, the Shrinerites trolled excommunicants with threats of hell, calling them liars and asking them how they lived with themselves after their betrayal.

Imagine waking up one morning to find out that everyone on your Facebook feed hates you and is calling you lying CIA scum married to a reptilian. It must play like a joke at first, though when you've been around it as long as Mike had, you know it is not. You yourself have been part of the hate-filled mob before.

Mike was lost. What could he do, but carry on? He put down his head and continued making orgone, though with less enthusiasm than in the past.

Now I don't know how long it took him to make the connection, but apparently one day it occurred to Mike that Brother Rich might not be dead. After all, Mike was sure his own wife was a human being and that he hadn't received any CIA training or paychecks. What if Brother Rich hadn't either? If that was the case, Brother Rich was owed an apology.

Mike contacted Rich, who welcomed him into a loose affiliation of other excommunicated agents, reptilians, and infiltrators. These people loved orgone and Yah, but not Sherry Shriner. He could still connect with doomsday preppers, reptilian hunters, all sorts of characters whose live-action role-playing world we occupy. Mike still felt betrayed, but he also saw a way forward without Sherry Shriner.

The pattern is undeniable and a little obvious. As I tried to get a handle on why and how Sherry Shriner operated the way she did, I uncovered maybe a dozen stories about dispatched followers. Sherry must be under constant attack to keep people engaged. Her choice of victim in these internal bloodlettings might seem capricious, but I think I may have noticed a through line.

Independent thought is the worst sin in Truther circles, though they claim it's what they prize most. The number of people who were outraged that Mike had called them lemmings wasn't as surprising as their public rebuttals, like, "I don't follow the crowd, I follow Sherry Shriner." They may have a point. In their lives, they're on their own path investigating things that most lemmings never even consider. Sherry just happened to be the best at it, so they joined her on her journey. For them, absolute faith in Sherry isn't like just following the crowd. But seeing the way Mike reached out to and embraced the other jilted members provides some insight into what makes Sherry Shriner a different kind of cult leader.

One of my takeaways from speaking to Shrinerites and other fringe evangelical sects was how they behave like the churches they despise. That is, they have rules for participation and inclusion, but they can be capricious. Think about divorced Catholics or kosher-keeping Jewish people who indulge in the occasional cheeseburger. Religious hypocrisy is a shaded scale that I'm not sure we've been looking at in the right way.

Very few people believe everything their religion claims. They just believe enough of it that they would rather be in the church than not. It's a tie to family, friends, and a wider spiritual life, even if you do have the occasional pepperoni pizza on a Lenten Friday. When people change churches or religions, it's because the rules for participation require too much of them. I don't think this is a novel insight, but when applied to Sherry Shriner, it takes on a different dimension.

The demand that a follower cut ties with friends and family who don't believe is a hallmark of a cult leader. In a normal cult, that makes sense. It is a disincentive for a person to leave or even to question the leader. Once the cult becomes their whole world, many people can't bring themselves to leave. Even if they haven't cut themselves off from their friends and family, some will endure almost anything rather than admit they were wrong or misled.

Sherry did all of those things, but she also jettisoned followers without warrant or notice. She encouraged intrigues that led to spiritual executions. Moreover, Sherry was surrounded by sycophants competing to show her the most support.

If someone made an off-message post or a too-blunt dissenting comment, senior members took offense on Sherry's behalf. They'd bring her cases of supposed transgressions and wait to see what she did. More often than not, Sherry would be dismissive. I know it's a little pat, but the atmosphere appears much like thugs trying to outdo one another and punctuating each new bold statement with, "Right, boss?"

Sherry loved the adoration, loved being able to take or leave it. Bestowing her attention or silence upon a comment could change the virtual weather in her Facebook chat room. Sometimes wounded, sometimes brazen, sometimes ecstatic, the tittering often began in her chat room as her show ended. Imagine groupies hearing the last song from the last encore and watching intently for the rock star to start the party.

After some shows, it was as if Sherry kicked the door in while holding two bottles of champagne. Alternatively, sometimes she would slide in and sulk, or endure the post-show praise because it was part of her job. The not knowing was part of the excitement, so responding to Sherry's entrance could get a person noticed, sometimes in a good way, sometimes not.

Sherry wasn't courting Christians so much as paranoia junkies. She understood that while she could use the conspiracy du jour to keep her addicts jumping, the hook was to stoke their paranoia in a personal way, to make it so they haven't just heard about secret government infiltrations, but that they've also been a target of them.

* * *

Reading what Marianne had to say about Richard a year after his alleged death set the tone for me. It helped me better understand what was going on behind the scenes when Kelly died, and how Shrinerites felt about their relationships with one another:

Kelly was conflicted—even though she was a super soldier Kelly turned on her handlers to help Sherry find 'brains' etc which were crucial/beneficial to [Lucifer] destroying mankind ... Kelly was just a kid ... tptb [The Powers That Be] & Kelly's mother and brother killed her off in December 2012 because Kelly refused to give Sherry poisoned food ... Now even though Kelly was a butt head thinking she should run stuff, she did more good than bad. Rich Brown was a cool and fun dude. The Rich Brown on face book now is a white dude prob FBI also. Rich thought he was slick and could play Sherry and get information. Sherry always sensed the serpent Rich was indwelled with ... Also whenever Rich went on missions with us he absolutely hated Kelly because she rode with Sherry and Rich went with me.

I can't imagine being accused by some internet troll of helping murder my daughter. More than that, though, I can't imagine the absolute lack of empathy. The arrogance mixed with impotent loneliness that turns middle-aged housewives into super soldier-thwarting operatives, and the depth of denial it takes to support that lie.

I don't know whether Marianne believed what she said so much as she found it less odious than admitting she'd spent a decade and a fortune supporting a fraud. Facing a reality where your life is gray and shitty is a distant second to one where you're a general in God's army. Attacking a dead girl's family is a small price to pay to support that reality.

Later in the conversation, Marianne wondered whether Rich's wife and family also were killed or were spared, or whether they were living with a clone and knew it or couldn't tell the difference. Brother Rich and Kelly were safe harbor for making up stories since they were both dead (Rich having been replaced by a clone). It kept conversation from lagging.

Then things got interesting.

Someone wondered if, as a spy, Richard made bad orgone, implying that some of the orgone Sherry had sold might be tainted. The prophet quashed it: Richard never made orgone, she said, he couldn't because he lived in a condo. He only went on missions. If she had any sense of irony, Sherry might have regretted inventing negative orgone energy when she accused Don Croft and other New Agers of making bad orgone. Instead, she just lied about Richard's orgone production just as she had lied about his death.

Of course, Brother Rich made orgone. He talked about it all the time, making it on his patio and how his wife hated the stench. He also helped make the orgone henge (think Stonehenge, but smaller) in Sherry's yard. In fact, it wouldn't shock me to discover he had a hand in refining the way to make what the Shrinerites called "our" orgone. Once asked and answered among the Shrinerites, the question was off the table, but among the expelled, the people who had seen Sherry for the intrigue-loving, self-promoter that she was, negative orgone was a real threat they lived with daily.

As Mike Hall and Brother Rich reconnected, and 2016 turned to 2017, the final act of Sherry Shriner, Queen of Heaven, was about to play out.

12

IF THERE ARE ANY ALIENS, TIME TRAVELERS, SLIDERS, OR ESPERS HERE, COME JOIN ME.

While neither woman would welcome the comparison, it's hard not to notice similarities between Shrinerites MJ and Barbara Rogers—both in their early forties, with fair skin and black hair, both worldly. They've been married and had relationships and adventures, and as it turned out, they both had a thing for Steven Mineo.

Barbara Hellen Rogers had packed a significant amount of living into her forty-two years. She'd been married and had a couple of kids in their late teens from whom she lived apart. She spent eight years in the Army before her bipolar disorder was severe enough to merit a medical discharge with a full pension. The upshot was she had cash and no pressing responsibilities. Although she was in touch with her kids, Barbara didn't have much to do but party, and it seems she was good at it.

Prior to 2017, her only real run-in with the cops was a drunk and disorderly charge in Miami more than a decade before, which, for me, calls up its own picture of a party girl goading the police into arresting her. But it could just as well have been that she was too rowdy. The point is, Barbara liked to drink and could afford to.

She said she met Steven online through Sherry Shriner. This is entirely possible. In fact, I imagine Steven contacted her the same way he contacted MJ, flirting at a distance with the most attractive single women on Sherry's followers list. But being a follower didn't make Barbara a believer.

What's clear throughout this entire ordeal was that Barbara didn't care very much about the Shrinerites or their beliefs. She was never an active participant on Sherry's Facebook page—more a fringe player at best. But I don't think where they met matters too much, because after a few months of chatting online and probably some meetups, Barbara came from Florida to live with Steven and his parents in North Arlington, New Jersey, toward the end of 2016.

There's some debate about whether she wore out her welcome in the Mineo household or if heading for the hills had always been the plan. Whichever the case, Barbara and Steven packed up her car and headed for their new home in the Poconos in February 2017.

Although it's part of the touristy Poconos, Tobyhanna, Pennsylvania, has more in common with less populated rural mountain towns. Six thousand or so people carve out all levels of middle-class existence, with trailers bumping up against the occasional planned community. Driving around, I thought about my own town, a weird mix of poorly kept rentals, trailers, planned neighborhoods with variations on two or three house styles, and the occasional grand home that looks like the overdressed guy at the bar.

Everyone in Tobyhanna worked and made a go of it, but tenuously, with an understanding that the economic good times fade fast and bad times take their time passing. Barbara and Steven moved into what she would describe as a studio apartment. For me, that conjures up a block of buildings or maybe a chic basement somewhere. I'll describe it as the back half of a trailer. Toilet and tub in one room, everything else in the other.

The couple dumped their entire lives into this space. Barbara sat cross-legged in a moving day photo, clear-plastic drawers, garbage bags, and loose blankets stuffed ceiling high into the closet behind her. It's a candid photo, blurrier than it has to be, taken with a phone flash for lack of light.

When the walls were painted, they were done so without care or even enough paint. You can see the roller marks where the former white mottles the paint that's daring me not to call it sinus-infection green, and where it collides with the closet molding (there is no door) marking the hole in the wall where a person can cram their stuff. The molding is the wrong color brown, shiny and streaked, bleeding into the wall and managing to reveal the past two color choices, light and dark blue. A royal purple rolling bag leans against the wall popping with contrast and newness.

In the photo, Barbara looks down, smiling broadly, her black knit cap pulled down over her eyebrows. Her hands are in her lap with her wrist at an odd enough angle that it looks longer and much, much thinner than it ought, bringing attention to her papery skin, her face almost blue under her pastel lavender eyeshadow. She's wearing a cosplay anime top, the blue V-collar and cuffs trimmed in red ribbon over a white shirt. It's a cheap costume, made of felt and possibly that paper-cotton material used in disposable hospital gowns. On her right arm is the Red Armband of Leadership from Nagaru Tanigawa's *Light* novel series and its accompanying anime episodes.

There's no point in recounting the entire character description, but the fan page linked to the photo I found has a Haruhi quote that's almost too coincidental: "I have no interest in ordinary humans. If there are any aliens, time travelers, sliders or espers [ESP-ers] here, come join me. That is all."

There was a girlishness about her, as if she were engaged in some massive role-playing game called being grown-ups. I don't think that's far from the mark. It's tempting to attribute everything that happened in Tobyhanna to Barbara's mental health issues. I reject that take, but I can't dismiss her state of mind out of hand. There were a lot of prescription medications in that studio—medications Barbara said she didn't always take. It's baffling to imagine her mood swings, or to even call them that. In her chats with girlfriends and even with her children, Barbara was a leaf on a stream. The kind of person my mother would describe as a dishrag, harmless and good-natured, but without will.

She liked pleasing Steven, though, and she liked how crazy he was about her. The decade between them wasn't as much a problem as which decade was between them. Although Barbara was in her early forties and he in his early thirties, they had the emotional lives of a twenty-nine-year-old dating a nineteen-year-old. Neither of them was responsible, and neither knew that would be a problem.

Steven was something of a man-child, innocent in his ignorance. In the wake of a person's death, there is, and ought to be, a greater forgiveness in the people who knew them, flaws become quirks. His mother told me he didn't have much experience with girls and that he was sweet. In taking apart his final months, these descriptions lost a little of their shine. "Sweet" became a euphemism for "not bright and more than a little naive." Steven struggled with reading and with abstract concepts. He was quick to take offense and show anger—like a mall security guard who could cut it in neither the military nor police force, but knew all the jargon and had all the gear.

As I dove in, the picture that emerged was of a frustrated young man unable to negotiate the adult world of sex and relationships, who raged at his powerlessness to bend the world to his will, who almost but couldn't quite understand what was holding him back.

* * *

The car stopped and Steven jumped out. He scrambled up the low wall and into the graveyard. This was a place where Steven was a person of consequence. His actions had meaning.

While he loved orgone missions, flag missions exhilarated Steven. He unfurled a Second Revolution flag, the preferred flag of pseudo-revolutionaries. It's a Tea Party symbol indicating a hatred for what this once-great country has become and a longing to go back to better days. One of Steven's treasured joys was raising the flag on empty flagpoles, and the graveyard in the Belleville Dutch Reformed Church near his parents' home was one of his favorite places to do it.

The property has belonged to the church since the 1670s, and served as a lookout post during the Revolutionary War. There are more than sixty Revolutionary War soldiers interred there. While it would be wrong to call the graveyard well kept, you get the impression that once or twice a year someone rolls up their sleeves and gives it a good mow. Sometimes they even put up a couple of American flags, but that day the flags were missing. Steven would remedy that.

The pole couldn't have been much more than ten feet high, and Steven was a practiced vandal. He pressed a catch in the center, detaching the top. With the flagpole top tucked under his arm for stability, he attached his flag before reattaching the pole and sending his banner to the top.

As Steven scampered back to the car, I can imagine how happy and excited he was, how his heart beat and his stomach stayed a little nervous until the car was well away. There's an emphatic glee about him and his actions, as dark as whatever was going on over the internet, but more pure. This was a strike against the NWO in real life that validated Steven's internet life.

I'm not certain how long it took for people to notice the flag this time. According to the available Google Street View images, a similar one was up from July through August 2012, and another for a month or so in 2013, but he likely hoisted them more often than that. It makes sense that this was something of a ritual for Steven. It's also amusing to imagine the groundskeeper occasionally adding another Second Revolution flag to a box in the church basement.

The guerrilla incursion was an extraordinary day in the life of Steven Mineo. He and Barbara had been in Tobyhanna a little more than a month when Steven went back home to pick up some personal items they'd left behind, like his metal detector, and maybe to visit. Barbara didn't accompany him. Although she was terrified of driving long distances, this hesitance feels more like commentary on her strained relationship with Steven's parents. The thing is, Steven didn't have a license. He didn't even drive.

When Steven texted Barbara that he was nearly home, he asked her to leave a Crystal Pepsi (re-released briefly in 2016) outside for "my bro." Someone made the hour-and-change trip from North Arlington to Tobyhanna and back to pick him up. While it's possible that his brother, Charles, made the drive, Steven still had a few friends he was in touch with. Whoever it was, they didn't get invited inside after driving Steven around all day. Steven had a different life altogether in Tobyhanna. A private one for himself and his new wife.

Steven declared them married. He saw himself as a rebel and revolutionary, independent of state or federal rule. No one but God needed to approve of their union. Barbara changed her name from Rogers to Mineo on her Facebook page, and they went about introducing themselves as married.

Between Barbara's disability pay and Steven's income from salvage and resale, especially now that he had his metal detector, they were set, which amplifies the playhouse aspect of it all. It's like the best day of vacation every day, when you forget that you even have a job, let alone that you have to get back to it. I imagine them waking up late and staying up later, drinking, exploring aimlessly, going out to eat, or just heating something up and watching TV. Of course, when I project myself into an idealized day for Barbara and Steven, I do so as a civilian, not as an operative on the front lines of the impending apocalypse.

* * *

Two weeks after getting home from New Jersey, Steven was on another mission, and this time he had a true accomplice. The Tobyhanna Army Depot is the area's largest single employer and only a mile or so from the trailer. The pair drove out there on a mission to spread orgone right on the base. As a communications and logistics hub, the depot brims with satellite dishes and towers spreading who knows what, so getting orgone in there was imperative.

There's no question what the depot is as you drive up to it, even if you don't see all the signs. There are gates and guards, intimidating-looking walls with cameras on them, and, of course, all the satellite dishes. Steven said Barbara got them in with her military ID, and they were able to gift orgone all over the area. The military base is extensive, so Steven must have known he would have to keep going back, but if they bought a house, he could. He could have a garage especially for the task, just like Sherry did.

There's a photo of one of the pucks he made among the evidence I uncovered in this research. It's easy to imagine Steven working to get the shot just right, holding his phone in front of his face and moving the puck back and forth to get the focus. I don't know whether he was selling them or just gifting them, but there's a tag on the bottom embedded late in the orgone-baking process. The tag has the Second Revolution symbol, the stars and numerals white on a square black field. Below that a message and signature: "This Oregon puck is dedicated to Yahuah & Yahushuah. Made in the USA by Steve M Mineo & Barbara."

First off, you can't blame him for the "Oregon" typo. As a person who's been writing the word a lot, autocorrect is no friend to orgone. But what I love about the tag is its childishness. The tag appears to have been placed without a complete signature, so clippings of single words were added, ransom style. One slip said, "Made in the USA by Steve," tacked next to it a slip that said, "M Mineo" and finally "& Barbara."

Out of context, there's no telling what the photo is of. You can make out the copper wire embedded in the resin, but the resin itself is brown and glassy, reminiscent of the bottom of a beer bottle. He couldn't wait to brag to the group about the mission on the depot.

He got a little praise, but Sherry was silent on the matter. Sherry was the one Steven wanted to impress. He'd asked her to let Barbara join Sherry's private Facebook chat in early March, and Sherry relented. Barbara didn't participate (although she read a lot of the chats), and Sherry rarely allowed strangers in, so this was something Steven wanted for himself. He liked to mention Barbara when he could. He seemed desperate for his old family to get along with his new one. Even if his biological family didn't like his new wife, if his fellow orgone warriors were on board, Steven would be satisfied.

It was March 24 when Steven celebrated his and Barbara's victory at the Tobyhanna Army Depot. It was simple, nothing, but debuting themselves as an orgone warrior couple may have caused the minor tectonic shift that set the first domino tumbling.

* * *

For the most part, MJ avoided contact with Steven once he lobbied to get Barbara admitted to the group. She told me he seemed happy and that she wasn't the kind of person who would interfere with someone's happiness. Her comments for most of the year were limited to congratulating Sherry on a good show or some variation of that. Quick in and out of the Facebook chat, although she continued to post on Sherry's public page.

The day after Steven told everyone about how he and Barbara orgoned a military base, MJ lobbed a lament into a discussion about how often people dismissed Sherry's claims and, by extension, her followers.

"Yeah, that's why I feel incredibly alienated from society. I can no longer live a normal life. Not like 'normal life' was ever any good anyway," she posted. "People bore me anger me annoy me all at once. I'm the only one like me in my area and I'm ready to die. Seriously. I want to go home."

A fellow Shrinerite, a Nigerian named Ubaka Peter, consoled her, reminding her that there was a war on. It was only natural for Satan to intensify his attacks and try to get the faithful to give up the fight.

"I wish you were living in my area, Ubaka," she told him. "You're super cool. We could hang out a lot. Talk. Get married, lol. You could help me with my henge and make orgone. It'd be perfect!"

Ubaka replied with a Facebook "sticker," a stick figure holding a huge red heart, as a sign of comfort and friendship.

"Yeah, but it's still lonely," MJ told him.

"It will pass."

"It hasn't passed and it has been 44 years."

* * *

Steven had someone to make an orgone henge with him, someone to go on missions, someone who'd never call his beliefs crazy, who wouldn't mock. Once when I was on the phone with MJ, someone knocked on her door. She excused herself to answer it. The voice had a much less refined Southern accent than hers, gruffer, cruder, an old man's voice. He was asking to borrow a book, something easy and small, that explained all the things MJ had been speaking to him about. He promised to bring it back.

It turned out it was a former classmate of hers, a man in his mid-forties who dropped out of school in the eighth grade. He had come by earlier in the day because he had heard she had gone crazy—that was the word among the neighbors. He found her out in front of her house trying to fix her broken mailbox and offered to do it for her.

MJ told me at the time that, while she was waiting to go home, which is how Shrinerites refer both to natural death as well as the aftermath of the impending apocalypse, it was nice to be able to open a few more eyes. Her enthusiasm was a glimpse into her isolation.

No one is going to elect me president of my neighborhood, but they don't whisper about how I'm a crazy person. It's okay if people think you're a jerk or a loudmouth or nosy. Those don't get whispers, but nobody wants to be the crazy lady down the block.

A few weeks after her conversation with Ubaka, MJ was poisoned. She suspected it was the wine, but when they're poisoning you, it's hard to know for sure. Steven reached out and let her know he was praying for her. That was all. She thanked him and let it go. But she kept getting sick and asking for prayers and support.

Then, in early May of 2017, Beverly reached out with some news:

"Hello Warriors just got a call from MJ," she said. "Please she needs our prayers right now ok something was attacking her and as I was trying to talk to her the phone went dead. Please pray for her right now. Thank you Yah bless!"

"Omg! What happened? Was she attacked?" Steven asked. "Does she have a firearm in the house?"

As always with the Shrinerites, there are independent accounts to go with the two realities. MJ put up a prayer shield to protect herself from attack, but she started choking anyway. On a phone call, she could hear Beverly's voice, but couldn't respond. Still, she locked in on her friend's words as a focal point to stay conscious. Help was too far away, so MJ decided to drive herself to the hospital. That's when she called Beverly a second time, knowing that her friend's voice would pull her through.

MJ was able to get out of the car and start breathing again as she made her way into the emergency room. It was the worst spiritual attack she'd ever experienced. She was drained, on painkillers and antibiotics, and unbelievably grateful for the work her fellow warriors did to help pull her through.

"I love you, my warrior family," MJ told them. "I felt alone but you were there for me. I love you all so much."

The other explanation, the one from this reality, is that she had an abscess that was too long unattended, and it made her very, very sick. She recently had been for a root canal, she said, and the procedure didn't go well. This cleared everything up for the older, wiser Shrinerites.

Sherry reminded MJ that they insert an ID chip inside your tooth when they do a root canal. She recommended a special magnet that MJ could put on the side of her face to deactivate the chip. Prevailing wisdom was if you have a dental problem, have the offending tooth yanked; it is the only way to prevent unwanted chipping.

Steven agreed.

"I have a crack in one of my teeth, but I refuse to go to the dentist because of that whole chips in the filling," he wrote. "That's why I just buy that dollar filling at the dollar store."

Over the next few weeks, as MJ was physically and spiritually nursed back to health, tension arose between her and Barbara, who watched the drama unfold without comment. It was a mutual, nameless jealousy that seethed deep. Something they both knew without speaking. MJ's complaints about loneliness followed Barbara's arrival and victory at the Army base. Steven's response and concern over MJ's recovery didn't go unnoticed by Barbara. Not long after, the death threats started.

4/17/2017 SHOW HIGHLIGHTS
ALWAYS HIDING STUFF BLACKENING OUT SKIES AT NIGHT

HEAVEN IS NOT JUST CLOUDS AND HARPS
NOTHING NEW UNDER THE SUN -
SOCIETIES ON ALL PLANETS
DIFFERENT GROUPS OF ANGELS THAT GROUP INTO
DIFFERENT COMMUNITIES
ANGELS HAVE FAMILIES (MAYBE ONE GROUP CAN'T
HAVE SEX)
HYBRIDS HAVE EXTREME IQ'S TRIPLE DIGIT IQ'S
HYBRIDS HAVE DIFFERENT AND OR EXTRA ABILITIES
ASTRAL PROJECTION DOESN'T CAUSE HYBRIDS
TO AGE LIKE IT DOES TO HUMANS

LUCIFER SET UP GIVE TO GET SYSTEM
TOOK MUSIC FROM HEAVEN & WORDS
CHANGED

BIBLE CODES ALWAYS HAVE 3 DIFFERENT
ROUTES FREE WILL CAN CHANGE THINGS

DIFFERENT GROUPS AND BRANCHES OF
SAME TREE IN HEAVEN
DIFFERENT STATUS'S IN HEAVEN (CAN
WORK WAY UP) - RULER OVER MANY THINGS
SPACE TRAVEL AND SPACE WEAPONS IN HEAVEN

A surviving screenshot from one of the websites Sherry maintained as she conducted her ministry.

An orgone pendant like the one Kelly wore. They were selling at the time for about $40 each.

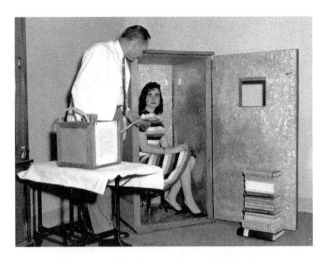

An example of one of Wilhelm Reich's orgone accumulators. Even though his theories were thoroughly debunked, variations on them are still available today. Photo courtesy of the US Food and Drug Administration, Public domain, via Wikimedia Commons.

A collection of orgone made for gifting and distribution by an unidentified Shrinerite.

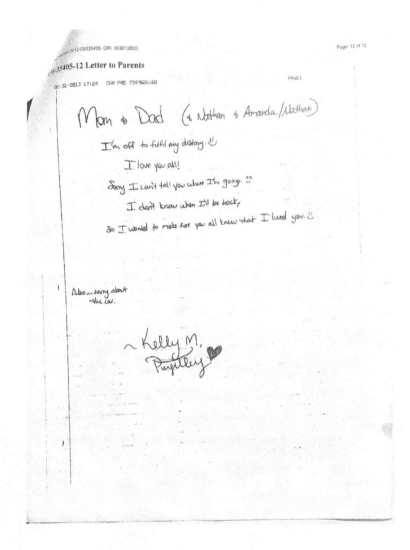

Mon & Dad (+ Nathan + Amanda/Nathan)

I'm off to fulfil my destiny. :)

I love you all!

Sorry I can't tell you where I'm going. :(

I don't know when I'll be back,

so I wanted to make sure you all knew that I loved you. :)

Also... sorry about the car.

~ Kelly M. Pingilley

A copy of the suicide note Kelly Pingilley left for her family. The police would find another one for her mother in the car that said, "Sorry for not calling."

Barbara Rogers moved into the studio where she and Steven lived at the time of his death.

Steven hoists the Second Revolution flag outside the Belleville Dutch Reformed Church, Belleville, NJ, in March 2017.

Barbara and Steven in their apartment after winning headphones in a claw machine game.

Steven made orgone pucks like these and tagged them for distribution. The misspelling "Oregon" appears to be unintentional.

Barbara Mineo
April 10 at 4:51am · 🌐

This is the best thing ever with cut up minced garlic. I just crave raw meat all the time for some reason. I know some are grossed out by it. But its a delicacy for me

👍😮 2   1 Comment

👍 Like   💬 Comment   ➤ Share

Barbara's original post about steak tartare. Sherry cited this appetite for raw meat as proof Steven had fallen into the clutches of a witch.

13

BRING IT ON, SCUMBAGS!
WAR IS HEATING UP.

Steven and Barbara may have had a passionate relationship, but it wasn't a healthy one. All they had was mutual physical attraction and a disdain for responsibilities. They were play-acting.

Steven was the revolutionary, on the run, under siege, and in constant danger. Barbara was the older woman, indulging him like a child while needing him to be in charge, to protect her and make everything all right. It was a role Steven embraced whenever he got the chance. He might not have been the breadwinner, but he was damn sure going to be the protector.

Not long after arriving in Tobyhanna, Steven worried that a German woman identifying herself as Luci Dicey Boatman was scamming Barbara. I don't know if this is a real person, but she was asking on behalf of "Silke Boatman," to whom Barbara had sent money before. Luci said she needed $150 to get Silke out of jail. That's when Steven stepped in, responding to the request with a video missive he sent to her over Facebook Messenger. Steven appears confident in the video, looking directly at the camera to deliver a mostly rehearsed speech. He doesn't grapple for words as he does in other extended messages.

Steven began it as he did many of his videos, "Incoming transmission!" He smiles and speaks pleasantly but without warmth, like a police officer saying "Sir" or "Ma'am" during an arrest. "How you doin'? I am Steve, I am Barbara's husband." Steven tells the person that he's just looking out for his wife's well-being, and goes on to say, "From the intelligence I seen on you, I believe that you are pretending to be other people."

Dressed all in dark blue: ball cap, windbreaker, and T-shirt, he's wearing four days' growth on his neck and upper lip, cultivating a rugged operator-in-the-field persona. His Roman nose is a little sharper than in his photos as he stares clear-eyed into the camera. Over his right shoulder, a Second Revolution flag juts diagonally from the top corner of what could be an armoire. He's trying to appear sympathetic. If there's a need, he said, their hearts go out to her, but Barbara won't be sending any more money.

He signed off: "God bless, end of transmission," and gave himself a frown of approval as if to say, "not bad," as he looked from the lens to the stop button.

And so they cruised through their lives, Barbara financing the day-to-day operations, giving Steven the money and permission he needed to feel like a revolutionary, Steven providing the confidence and ability to deal with the outside world. They believed their relationship would continue forever, but they also believed the government was run by reptilians.

In truth, when that faith was tested, it would crack and end their world. The first test came a little before midnight Friday, May 19, when a troll visited Steven's Facebook page.

Steven posted a video they didn't want you to see of people being forced to turn in their guns. Screen name "Rob Roberts" wrote: "u don't have a gun" to which Steven's typed reply said something along the lines of "come find out." The next day he got a message from "Chris Connell" with information that only could have come from inside Sherry's ranks. It read:

Ha ha ha ha we no who ur. We been watching u for 12 years. We are [Sherry's] friends......... We like to keep tabs on u cus we no u r a violent kid.......

we no where you live. We will get ur wife and feed her to The Queen
Shazuary.......

Steven was more angry than shaken, at first. He invited the
troll to come by and have a "good old skirmish."

"Keep this up and i will report this. And do not think they
can't find out were you live," he wrote. Then, "AND DON'T CALL
ME A KID YOU PIECE OF TRASH."

Steven was quick-tempered when it came to Barbara, but he
also was afraid beyond his baseline paranoia. It's the difference
between believing "they" are out to get you and having proof. After
all, it was well known that the New World Order constantly infiltrated Sherry's ranks, and this troll knew Sherry's "Angel" name,
Shazurazy, even if they didn't get the spelling quite right. Steven
had to warn the other orgone warriors that they had an infiltrator.
It was late, but there usually was someone around. Steven retold
the story and then started the comment thread.

"Whoever was posting that I'm praying for the equipment
they used to be disabled Beyond recovery and repair and immediate Judgement if they try anything," Steven wrote. "It would be
so hilarious if yahuah destroyed their equipment lol."

"I hope he does, I just prayed it to happen," someone
responded. "And that he gets a flat tire. Just a little icing on the
cake."

There was more like that, silly, impotent curses that would
be cute if they weren't coming from adults. Someone in the chat
room pleaded with Sherry not to "eat Steve's wife," before the
prophet chimed in.

"am i the cookie monster," Sherry wrote.

Her followers thought it was the best quip they'd read in a
while. In light of everything that followed, though, this exchange
stuck with me as an oddity. Accusations that there was a spy
tended to get serious responses from Sherry. Ambivalence wasn't

her style. It didn't bother her that Steven uncovered an infiltrator. There were no calls for an investigation, no admonitions to be careful, no threats from the others in the group on Sherry's behalf about finding the traitor. Sherry's response was a green light for the attacks on Steven to continue. It was her way of saying, "You don't have my protection."

For me, this is the first inclination that Sherry might have already decided Steven Mineo's fate. He could have Barbara, but at the cost of being a serious member of the group. Sherry understood Barbara wasn't interested in her ministry in a way that Steven was blind to. Going along on orgone missions didn't make her an orgone warrior. She hadn't committed a dime to the ministry, and hadn't even chimed in to thank Sherry for her wisdom or to seek it in confidence. All Barbara had done was tempt one of her premier warriors with an eye on leading him astray.

Of course, no one leaves Sherry's ministry unless they're expelled from it. What Sherry didn't understand, what she never could understand, was Steven's vision for the future. He envisioned a time where Barbara would be as enthralled with orgone as he. By the time he learned he could no longer trust Sherry or the other orgone warriors, he would be too far gone to handle the consequences. Like his mom said, he was a sweet kid.

* * *

It helps me to think of Sherry's Facebook chat room as a literal drawing room, Victorian furniture, books on shelves, a south-facing row of windows with white curtains. Everything is blurry, to signify that it isn't the real world. People come and go, speak together within earshot of the others who sometimes will chime in and other times remain disengaged.

Visiting the chat room in its frozen past, I watched the conversations unfold like Scrooge in *A Christmas Carol*, understanding their import and powerless to alter their course. The content of the crosstalk only heightened the unreality. It's where I came to understand that these people were not bluffing.

Facebook is often a place where people say awful things they don't mean in their heart. Sometimes it's bluster, other times it's tin-eared humor or hyper-contrarianism. Sherry's chat room had none of this ugliness. The ugliness in her room was deeper because it was true. I observed people who knew the implications of their words and said them anyway.

Once, Steven had popped on to speculate about a recent movement in cryptocurrencies, which many in the conspiracy community have turned to as part of their belief in NESARA. As he made his case, it was easy to see the attraction, first of bitcoin and then the lesser-known cryptocurrencies, as related to the persistent belief that the United States economic system is on the brink of collapse.

These aren't people investing in an alternate currency as a hedge against a weaker dollar. They are stocking up for the day when dollars (or any country's currency) are worthless. With so many of the people I've spoken with or researched, no plan is ever for a rainy day. It is all for the end of the world. These aren't economists, so it isn't shocking that their apocalyptic scenario includes a battle with Lucifer and the abolishment of the state, but also a functioning internet and electrical grid with participation limited to the people that bought, say, Dogecoin right before the end of the world.

The premise is that when doomsday comes, the people who wouldn't listen to them, who mocked and ostracized them, will be sorry. Not just about failing to invest in cryptocurrency, but in ignoring all the other signs Sherry had been revealing for years.

Every day the world doesn't end is another disappointment. Every disappointment grows their anger and strengthens their resolve. This charade goes on for decades for many, and as the years pass, they don't make any effort at all to ask why they want the world to end or where the pre-schadenfreude comes from.

That's what compels me so about this world view. Take a guy like Steven. He might be good with machines but he's no physicist, yet he and the other Shrinerites operate in a world where the CIA just can't neutralize them. The world's top assassins have tried and failed to kill Sherry Shriner, and as we've seen, many, if not most of them, have stories about evading or duping some of the best operatives thousands of years of warfare and subterfuge have produced.

I understand the premise. God is protecting them because they're making orgone and keeping it close. What's difficult to accept is how orgone fails some people. People like Kelly who, although her home was filled with orgone, wasn't protected enough to keep her mother and brother from dragging her out of bed in the middle of the night, screaming as they killed her before driving her body to a remote place, writing fake suicide notes, and dumping her.

Orgone didn't protect Mike Hall who, despite spending thousands of dollars for the production and support of Sherry's orgone ministry, had been living with a reptilian for years, and who had made a life with this person who was just using him to spy on Sherry Shriner. It didn't protect Brother Rich, whose horrible death and betrayal at the hands of his FBI handler remain lore to this day.

Orgone also was about to fail Steven Mineo. And like all of the exiled Shrinerites before him, the realization that orgone was a mere spiritual placebo would be too much for him to accept.

* * *

"I have a very serious problem guys," Steven wrote as if he had just burst into the chat room, breathless. "I just got a unusual text. I'll send it to you now. I'm going to need everybody's prayers immediately for Me and Barbara."

Sherry's chat room was quiet. It was after 3:00 a.m. Monday, May 22. I watched as Steven wrote and posted into the silence, knowing he would be heard once people started checking their phones and not waiting for a reply. There had been another death threat. This time it included a picture of his and Barbara's home. Someone was stalking him. Worse, someone was stalking Barbara. He posted a few screenshots of the Facebook message.

"When we get you we are going to feed your wife to the queen Sherry"

"PRAISE THE QUEEN OF HEAVEN SHERRY"

"The Queen Shaz needs to drink ur pure blood"

"Don't u no who Sherry really is?"

"Ha hahahaha"

"We tracked u down using orgone…Ur orgone is a GPS signal. PRAISE SHAZAURY FOREVER Sherry and us will drink of ur blood soon."

Next to each post was the leering visage of a gray alien. Objectively, the figure in the photo was passive, huge expressionless eyes and only a nearly crooked mouth, the right corner higher as if the alien had been the victim of a mild stroke. But next to the words, maniacal and sometimes in all caps, it's easy to superimpose emotion on the dead face. It looks snarky and mean.

Interspersed among several of the comments were photos of the home on Laurel Drive Steven and Barbara shared. The message had been sent a little after 4:30 Saturday morning, not long after Steven had told the others he had gotten into it with the troll he had invited to "skirmish." That he hadn't noticed makes sense. When you message a stranger on Facebook, they don't get a notification. Instead, there's a link that says, "Message Requests." If you click, you'll see whether anyone who isn't already a friend tried to contact you.

Steven was at a loss for how to respond. Someone in Sherry's camp knew where he lived and was out to get him. He needed the prophet's counsel and support.

Steven waited ten minutes, and then he asked Barbara if he should call the police. What would he tell them? That aliens were threatening to eat his wife? If you or I were to get messages like that, we'd be disturbed. How could we not be? But imagine the raw fear when you inhabit Sherry Shriner's reality where aliens do collect and eat people. Sherry preached often, and at length, about people being disappeared to NWO slaughterhouses and reintegrated into the food supply.

Although it only took Sherry twenty or so minutes to wander into her chat room, when she did, Steven didn't get the relief he was hoping for. Instead, he got a small taste of what was to come.

* * *

"Bring It On scumbags! War is heating up." The most recent of Steven's comments lay flat on the screen that glowed blue in the predawn quiet. When Sherry responded, she was not alarmed or even surprised.

"That is crazy," she said. "Why would they go after you and no one else?"

Steven didn't take the hint. In his mind, it was obvious. They came after him because of all the important work he was doing with Barbara. They were going on missions all the time. Steven had promised God that if he was granted a wife, the couple would praise Him and spread His orgone. God had granted his wish, and Steven was paying his debt so well it was making Lucifer nervous.

"I take it as a badge of honor," he wrote.

Sherry shared some of her hate mail stories with him and told him not to worry.

"Just set warrior angels around there," she told Steven. "Dad's not going to let them do anything."

The rest of her advice was similar: tell them you're represented by The Most High and they'll be thrown into hell with chains if they mess with you. Mostly she told him not to be afraid. He assured her he wasn't.

"I was laughing when I read the email," he wrote in response to Sherry's post. "I just want Barbara to feel okay."

In our reality, Steven called the police. Patrolman Jesse Bohrman (whose father, Detective John Bohrman, would investigate Steven's death) showed up and took his statement, got copies of the messages, and tried to put Steven's mind at ease. The photos were from Google maps, just screen captures from someone who had his address. That did little to ease Steven's mind.

Over the ensuing weeks, Steven and Barbara each worried they weren't doing enough to keep their spouse from breaking down. As the final drama of Steven's life played out, the two adult children playing house would have to guess at what real grown-ups would do. Each understood they had to protect the emotional well-being of the other, but didn't know how. The best they could manage was to hope it solved itself.

Steven and Barbara weren't problem solvers. They were buck passers. In their minds, things happened to them because of outside forces. Other people, the government, the devil, all contributed to the tumult that beset them. Of course, in this case, that happened to be true, but so focused were they on their persecution from without, they never connected their past trials with the ones that were to come.

The "wheres" and "whys" of this first attack on Steven and Barbara don't have any pleasant answers. I know I didn't write the threats, and I'm pretty sure Steven didn't send them to himself. When I spoke with MJ, she flat-out denied sending it and seemed almost confused by the question. Sherry could have sent it. She used the gray alien photo on an Obama meme in 2013, and she had Steven's address. I just don't know why she would.

For a time, I considered whether Barbara might have sent it as a perverse joke or maybe even to show Steven how dumb it looked, but she was bothered enough by the messages to ask her daughter's advice and to entertain her invitation to come visit. Plus, Steven used her phone a lot and would have seen the posts there if she had sent them.

My budding conspiracy theorist brain keeps pointing out that *Shazurazy* was misspelled, but that's not a mistake anyone who knew Sherry's angel-name would make—on purpose, anyway. In the end, it wouldn't matter to Steven or Barbara because things were going to get a lot worse. When they did, neither would have the capacity to tie this first attack to the rest, but it was the beginning of the end of their relationship with Sherry Shriner.

14

I SENSE WE STILL HAVE LEAKS . . . THEY WILL BE OUTED.

It had been a fraught twenty-four hours, and Barbara and Steven decided to go out to dinner and blow off some steam. Steven liked to go to the casino, but mustn't have been too lucky, which seemed to be a minor source of disagreement. Maybe Barbara didn't feel they had the budget to support regular trips there, but nights out for food and drinks were a luxury they maintained.

I don't think Lombardi's Brookside Tavern is quite a quarter mile from where Barbara and Steven lived. It's a short walk, and one they liked to take. Like Tobyhanna itself, Lombardi's wasn't there to cater to the tourists. The few times I was there everyone was nice, but I reeked of "outsider" among the other 2:00 p.m. patrons.

The converted house has a clubby feel. Red, white, and blue promotional flags weathered to ghosts hang from the aging wooden fence that sets off the backyard. Some had thinned to translucence, and I wondered, as I always do, whether it bothered any of the red-blooded Americans who came to sit in the yard, which is a destination in itself.

An outdoor bar, complete with an overhang for protection from the sun and tiled in beige marblesque block, takes a small corner of the cement patio running north the length of the property. The yard proper includes a pair of horseshoe pits and a substantial fire ring for those cold Pennsylvania nights. Or any night, really.

Lombardi's has a long, broad front porch with a lonely plastic chair next to one of those wide-bottomed, long-necked cigarette-disposal contraptions, which is a sad country song all on its own. The house door reminds bikers that while they are welcome, their colors are not.

Inside, I sat at the bar next to a man with a brand-new face tattoo who couldn't have been too far away from his seventieth birthday in either direction. I hoped the rumor about teardrops representing murder victims was just that, because they were streaming down his right cheek. It could have been my own prejudice that bothered me, but as I thought about what it would be like to be a regular here, I wondered how many beers I'd need before I could ask about the "no colors" sign and what prompted it. More than two, I guess.

The bar itself is light and polished, running the length of what might have once been the living room and cutting off at an area that could have been a den and mudroom. A sliding glass door occupies the back wall, and an ordinary one the far right corner. Think of it as a utility entertainment area with a couple of arcade games, including one of those claw prize machines, a dance floor, and a small space used by karaoke hosts and bands accustomed to claustrophobic conditions. Folding chairs sat in a neat row next to the door, presumably for expanded seating outside.

To the left of the bar, what might have been the dining room is, well, a dining area with pizza parlor seating and access to the bathrooms. There are windows everywhere so during the day it may as well be an Applebee's, but at night there's no question it's a real bar. I wasn't there at night, but Barbara and Steven were. They were new people in this small town biker bar, and neither was gregarious.

I imagine them staring ahead at one of the televisions mounted on the wall or working their phones. Killing time, chatting, and eating. I wonder about the conversation, whether they talked about the end times and how Steven was preparing, or whether he regaled her with insights from the most recent Sherry Shriner show, or talked up his newest YouTube video. When you spend every waking moment together, there's not a lot to catch up on except recounting your digital day.

I don't know if it was the whim Steven claimed it was or whether playing the claw machine was a trade-off for not going to the casino that evening, but Steven took fifty cents over to the massive arcade-style prize machine. Barbara joined him. Steven said a prayer, asking God to let him win that pair of headphones he had his eye on. He worked the joystick, trying to maneuver the claw into just the right position. I've always thought of these machines as double cons. Sure, some people win out of sheer dumb luck, but savvy players (according to YouTube) know they're being cheated and use the machine's chicanery against it, an "honor among thieves" approach where, by cheating just the right way, you win honestly.

Whether through his mechanical inclination or divine intervention, Steven was able to yank the headphone box free from the pile and drop it into the prize bucket. He was ecstatic. If they weren't chatty with the bar patrons before, they were a little now. Steven was a winner. God had selected him to receive those headphones, and he wanted to tell people about it.

Steven said the manager came over and asked if she could take his picture with the headphones to show her boss, but I'm under the impression that he was bragging to her before the notion crossed her mind. He took a picture of his prize to share with the group.

"Hey everyone check this out just for fun I asked Yahuah to let me win this $0.50 machine prize," he wrote in Sherry's Facebook chat room.

It was not quite 11:30 p.m., though, and the post didn't get much traction. No matter, he had his headphones, and he had his wife. They made their way out the door and back to their trailer. Whenever I made the walk, I stuck to the wrong side of the road, even during the day. I felt safer seeing the traffic before it passed me. There are no sidewalks, and the shoulders are too narrow in places. The streetlights are at highway distance, and I imagine Steven and Barbara in that weird purple light as they moved between illuminated circles, holding hands or arm in arm, drunkenly or just a little tipsily, making their way through Tobyhanna alone. Steven was still on cloud nine when they finally made it through the door. He couldn't wait to tell the chat room and took a smiling selfie—Steven in his headphones leaning in with Barbara.

It's a silly picture in that they look as if they're having a joke, but there's a sadness to it that isn't improved by knowing how the story ends. Just looking at their room depresses me. It's not that it's cheap and small, but rather there is a sliminess to it, a wet dinge that's amplified by the sinus wall and the chintzy, shoddily painted molding. The window looks as if it's been covered over with tape and whatever cardboard was lying around.

I'm not a snob nor was I above tacking up sheets where blinds ought to go when times were tough, but shiny tape on the windows radiates madness. Even when one person in the picture isn't much more than a month away from killing the other person in it. Barbara made it her profile picture, and that's when things started to get weird.

* * *

"This Raul Sanchez guy is clearly a Sherry Shriner hater." It was Ubaka Peter, the rabid Shrinerite MJ wished lived closer, reporting the Facebook page goings-on to members of the chat.

Sherry's page was atwitter over a post that proved giants existed. The post was a still from the 2007 comedy/sci-fi movie *Big Man Japan*. Jenna Wilford, another of Sherry's top generals, didn't argue whether or not it was from a movie, only that movies used real footage of giants to get people used to seeing them. It was an NWO psy-op. Sanchez had been an on-again, off-again thorn in Sherry's side for a while.

"He's a little punk I've kicked off my list before," Sherry said. "He uses fake names to get back on."

They called Raul's loyalty into question because he had interrupted Jenna while she was attacking a guy for saying the giant was from a movie.

"Oh, come on Jenna. Mr. Stone didn't disrespect her, he just disagreed with Sherry on this giant being real. Let's not be too harsh."

"Stone was DISRESPECTING our Sherry Shriner. And if you don't think so then you are on his boat." Jenna lost it, and it's worth noting that she did it a lot and continues doing so to this day. She persisted on the Facebook page attack and then stalked into the private chat room. "I sense we still have leaks … they will be outed."

It's not just Jenna's fanaticism, but also her newfound bloodlust that made me suspicious. She was instrumental in ousting Mike Hall and continues to threaten people who disrespect Sherry. As we see with Raul, disrespect includes failing to crucify people who show sympathy for dissenters. She may not have done what became the damning research into Barbara Rogers, but Jenna was one of the loudest voices of the persecution that followed.

Sometime on Tuesday, May 23, an old post of Barbara's made its way into Sherry Shriner's orbit. It was an April 10 photo of steak tartare (seasoned, raw ground beef served with a raw egg and sides of relishes) with a caption about how much Barbara liked raw meat and sometimes craved it.

It's possible Sherry found it scrolling idly down Barbara's Facebook page, but it makes more sense that it was presented to Sherry by an overenthusiastic or jealous follower. Maybe someone was jealous of Barbara or of Steven's rise to prominence as the member of an orgone gifting couple. Or maybe it was someone who thrives on drama and damnation, but the way Steven responded suggests Sherry was endorsing rather than leveling the accusation: Barbara was a blood-craving witch.

"She will destroy you," Sherry wrote, "So wake up and stop getting blinded by her, or get destroyed by her."

"Sherry, I have reason to believe you're just siding with the majority." Steven was baffled. "Please Don't block me. I think this is one big mistake. I'll get through this, our faith is strong with him."

He was already starting to feel reality shifting under his feet. Steven was in no way prepared to get a message like that. If you could have stopped that second in time, that moment before the message came through, and asked Steven what he believed, he would have told you he believed in Sherry Shriner, Daughter of The Most High, Queen of Heaven, and Yah's Prophet and Ambassador on Earth. He knew that in the way he knew orgone had supernatural powers and that he was standing in his studio apartment in Tobyhanna, Pennsylvania.

Bing. The message alert sounded.

It was a message from Sherry telling him that the other person in the room, the woman he called his wife and for whom he had forsaken all others, was an inhuman double agent bent on destroying all that is holy in the world.

If I were standing when I got that news, I'd make my way to the nearest chair. I might even reply "LOL" if I had my wits about me. We've all found out things we believed weren't true. We've suffered betrayals and minor schemes, waded through the confusion, trying to reorient ourselves. But few of us have ever been told that nothing we believe is true. This, in the end, would be Steven's undoing.

He had participated in a fantasy world for the better part of two decades, a world populated with super soldiers, giants, vampires, and evil overlord reptilians wearing people as if they were suits. All of it hinged on the word of a woman who had just told him his wife was a witch and to leave her. His first reaction was to ask the orgone warriors to pray that it wasn't true. They doubled down on their vitriol. Steven Mineo was lost.

* * *

Everything clicked for Steven at once. If Barbara wasn't a witch, Sherry was a liar. Steven couldn't conceive of that world even as the truth pressed against his consciousness. What if the 9/11 plot, martial law, economic collapse, orgone—what if none of it was real? He pushed the thought away.

Not possible.

There were only two alternatives: Sherry was mistaken, or he was in the room with a witch. To give you a sense of how seriously Steven took this possibility, he told Barbara they would prove that she wasn't a witch. Barbara must have been incredulous, but the fact that she endured it and that Steven conducted the test speaks volumes about their mental states. Remember, they had only been living together for six or seven months at this point and dating not much longer than that. This was a huge ask.

Barbara knew it was critical to placate Steven in all matters Sherry Shriner. This ranged from helping him make videos for her, to buying orgone material and baking the foul-smelling concoction to Sherry's specifications, to submitting to a literal humanity test. Worse than that, if she refused, it would be the same as confessing. That is the power of Sherry Shriner. Although they were hundreds of miles away from Sherry in Ohio, neither of them ever had a choice.

Steven sat Barbara down and prayed to Yahuah, asking him to prevent her from blocking the power of orgone in any way. As she listened to his earnest prayer, how strange must her life have seemed, looking at his face, eyes closed in concentration as he prayed, asking for protection from Barbara in this test, begging Yah to prevent her using supernatural powers to undermine this experiment.

Steven placed orgone on (and probably around) Barbara and waited for her to change. She didn't. Barbara didn't burn nor did she reveal her inner demon. She just sat there, feeling stupid as the anticlimax stretched into embarrassed silence. For her. Steven was invigorated, he couldn't wait to report the results to Sherry, but Barbara had another plan in mind.

Earlier that year, when Mike and Kristy Hall were accused, Barbara didn't unfriend them as the others had. Why would she? She didn't really believe in this reptile nonsense. Now the accusation started to sound familiar. Barbara messaged Mike to ask about his experience.

"If you don't mind me asking, what happened between you and Sherry Shriner? Did they accuse you of being CIA?" Barbara wrote.

The message lit up Mike Hall's darkness. After nearly a year without communication, someone from the group was talking to him again.

"Hey Barbara! No, I don't mind," Mike replied. "Ya, after 12 loyal years of following her ministry she and her lemmings accused me of being a CIA spy and my wife of being a reptilian and kicked us to the curb!"

Mike remembered his ouster. How it had toppled his world.

"So how did it happen for you guys? Did someone reach out to you and tell you this or were you guys verbally attacked?" he asked. "I woke up one day and signed into Facebook and noticed I was down about 30 or so friends and they were all part of the Sherry crowd. I was so confused as to why until a fellow friend filled me in on what they were saying about my wife and I."

From the first few moments of the flame war, Barbara was looking to end it peacefully and without conflict, the same way she submitted to the orgone test. Steven hoped for reconciliation, but Barbara only wanted a way out. The craziness was too much, and, besides, they didn't need the Shrinerites, they had one another. Steven didn't agree. He told Sherry about the successful orgone experiment and was sure Yah would let her see the truth.

"I don't believe that they are wicked people," Steven told Barbara. "Just a big mistake they're making. They need to go to Yahuah directly when it comes to the truth. I feel betrayed."

Sherry had dismissed his proof, claiming it only proved that Barbara was a stronger witch than she first had suspected. That's when Steven understood that there was no way back into Sherry's life or ministry. The only thing left for him was to try and burn the whole thing to the ground.

15

WE LOVE OUR ORGONE, MAN.

"This just got so much bigger for me once I realized who you were!" Mike was a little starstruck as Steven joined his conversation with Barbara. "And your wife is really cool by the way … I'm so glad she reached out to me!"

Steven's position as a warrior made his dismissal something of a scandal. Steven had orgoned the New York Super Bowl and made videos for Sherry that garnered hundreds of thousands of hits. If Mike was a foot soldier in the war, Steven was a commando, but now they had something in common. They built on that in their earliest voice messages to one another.

The conversation had a quiet, late-night feel. As Mike recounted his Sherry Shriner excommunication experience, they were just two guys talking about their lives and emotions over the phone and in the dark, getting as close to vulnerable as they're capable. Mike explained how he and Kristy rebuilt their lives. They still believed in Yah, the alien agenda, and the power of orgone; they still taught their children to believe, too, but felt alone, hurt. After burning bridges with his family over Sherry Shriner, he couldn't very well go back and endure people thinking he was crazy.

Steven also claimed that his family hated him for his beliefs. I don't know if that's true. As with so many cult members, it's easier to claim to be a victim than to admit that your family thinks your beliefs are stupid. It was the same with Kelly. Her family and friends didn't disown her for following Sherry. They just tried to show her that Sherry was a fraud, so Kelly avoided them. In her mind, they just didn't understand and needed her help and protection all the more.

Certainly, Steven's family wasn't nuts about Barbara, but there's no evidence that enmity extended to him. "I know the truth, and people just can't handle it" is neater, turning a self-imposed exile into a final imaginary persecution. Worse, the tension magnifies as family and friends struggle not to push a fanatic over the edge because they seem otherwise fine. Of course, they're not fine, and in a troubling, fundamental way.

The tragedy is Sherry and people like her understand their followers would rather endure fraudulence, lies, and bullying than admit that they're not central to God's plan for the imminent end of the world. They're as unremarkable as the rest of us, but some people would rather die than face that reality.

Steven didn't work hard to find out who dug up that raw meat post. It baffled me for a long time until I understood that he agreed with Sherry on some level. The photo was undeniable. Barbara said she craved raw meat. Who tattled on her wasn't Steven's issue. Throughout the ensuing back and forth, Steven referred to it as "Barbara's food post." Steven didn't have a clue about dietary prohibitions and how they worked. He didn't want to know. Instead, he just threw his energy into disproving Sherry's claims.

In recounting a bit of his discussion with Sherry, Steven told Mike that when the prophet first leveled her charges against Barbara, he asked the community to pray to The Most High that it wasn't true, that there was some mistake, and Barbara wasn't really a reptilian.

"She told me The Most High laughed. 'You're asking warfare warriors to pray?' And that was a red flag," he said. "I mean my poor wife was praying, like, 'Are you really laughing at me?' It's a really mental pain. It's really bad."

As he navigated the two realities, our shared one and Sherry Shriner's, Steven had to throw up more psychological walls just to keep from being crushed. He dared not think Sherry could be making this up. Not just that Barbara was a reptilian, but that there were such things as reptilians. Without reptilians there's no New World Order, and without the NWO there's no economic collapse and martial law. Everything he was preparing for was the joke people said it was. He deserved the looks of pity or disdain he got when people realized he was a Truther.

I'm reminded of children in those crucial years when they discover that we're lying to them about magical worlds. After they learn about the Tooth Fairy, the Easter Bunny isn't far behind, and from there the entire facade crumbles.

Even though it took Steven longer to come to terms with Sherry's lies than it probably ought, there was a similar progression in his last weeks. He wondered aloud whether orgone was real, or whether Sherry invented that as well, especially since without orgone there was no way to prove Barbara wasn't really a witch. Mike was there to reassure him for the time being, but Steven would spend most of the rest of his life searching for one last article of faith. Mike had seen orgone's miracles. If Steven couldn't trust Sherry, that was one thing, but orgone was unimpeachable from his point of view.

"I wear my pendant. My wife wears one, my two sons wear one. We love our orgone, man," Mike told Steven. "We fuckin' make it and spread it everywhere, and that's not going to change. Ever."

Mike was the smoking gun Steven hoped for, proof that Sherry lied. He would turn the facts of his own story, as well as Mike's, into a crusade: a documentary featuring clips and interviews debunking her teachings. He saw the possibilities and the horrors all at once. "Oh! She's good!" he told Mike.

"She says a lot of truth, like martial law and economic collapse, which is true," he said, landing hard on "true" as much for his psychological well-being as for emphasis. "But there's rat poison mixed up with it."

As with Mike, Steven believed that everything Sherry said was true except the lies, which were the things they didn't believe. Having spoken with Mike, Steven was ready to confront Sherry. She had her chance to recant her lies about Barbara and chose not to. Now Steven would make her pay.

"She said that The Most High said to her that, 'Not one of them will fall from his hands,' right?" Steven was getting his philosophical juices flowing and you could hear the excitement in his voice as he linked practice and belief together into an airtight metaphysical alibi. "Now Sherry is all of a sudden saying that Barbara could *destroy* me? Now everybody's saying I'm going to go to *hell*? That doesn't add up. It doesn't make sense. She's contradicting herself."

They decided something was off about Sherry that they couldn't understand. Steven and Mike were confident that Sherry was the problem, not orgone. Mike hypothesized that something happened to turn Sherry Shriner evil, and the true faithful were being tested. He, Steven, and the others were the wheat being separated from the chaff. Steven loved that idea. It was clear now that Sherry was the last obstacle to a personal relationship with Yah.

"I love The Most High so much! Isn't it awesome how he works!?" Steven told Mike as the entire plan dawned on him. "And now I know! You see the test was, 'If I take Sherry out of your life, are you still going to love me? Are you not going to want the gift I gave you?' "

Barbara wasn't the woman of Steven's dreams. She was the woman of his prayers. Sure, Kelly's death was evidence that the NWO was after Sherry, but each night when he went to bed,

Steven did so in the company of God's gift to him. Absolute proof that he had The Most High's favor and indulgence, that he was saved and protected. Everything he asked had been given through Barbara Rogers.

* * *

Just like that, Steven had a new religion. He was even more central to God's plan than he had dared imagine. As he understood it, first you had to accept Sherry's teachings, then you had to endure her betrayal. Once you came through it, you had to cast her away to prove your commitment. Mike was right. For whatever reason, Sherry was turning against her faithful, and it was time to make a stand. Steven took up his message from Sherry the night before, where he had asked her to reconsider and not side with the majority.

"Something's not right. What you're saying against Barbara is wrong. I did wake up and I caught you in your lie and you are trying desperately to cover it up," he told her. "You're now going back on what the Heavenly Father said."

In addition to having accused Mike Hall, Sherry had (through Beverly) told Steven that he was an Angel in the Flesh. She doubled down on the first and recanted the second.

"People that been supporting you for years you kick them to the curb," he wrote.

"Oh Shut up," she replied. "You're blinded."

"You're starting to sound like a false prophet!"

There wasn't much else after that. Steven left Sherry's Facebook chat room. Sherry removed Barbara the next day and canceled her show that night. Steven thought he spooked her, which must have given him a little pleasure. He wanted revenge. Not for all the time and money he wasted on Sherry, not for the deceit, but for the accusation and the embarrassment. Steven needed to prove he wasn't a loser.

Jenna chimed in on the heels of Sherry's messages, telling him, "You've got secrets, Steve."

He got similar messages from Beverly, threats of having secrets exposed. These threats told Steven more than he wanted to know about how Sherry's world worked. Steven knew he didn't have any secrets. Maybe he didn't know for a fact that Barbara wasn't a reptilian or that Sherry wasn't the Daughter of The Most High, but he did know his heart was pure. He knew he didn't have ties to the FBI or the CIA. He also knew that God had personally endorsed and consecrated his marriage. There was no chance he would abandon Barbara, even if she wasn't the one with the income, the car, and a plan for the future. Steven was mad about her, and very little would change that.

I'm not sure he could tell the difference between affection and obsession. He knew Barbara loved him and decided to make a very public statement by having her write to Sherry:

I just want you to know that you have hurt Steven really bad. I dont want to send you this message but he pressured me to do so. He has lived with me for 9 months and he has never seen me shape shift into a reptile or perform a crazy witch craft ritual. Steak Tartare (raw beef) is a popular dish in Europe, Your followers cant be that ignorant and I like exotic food. Steve would definitely know if I was a witch or a reptile. By now he would have left me. Anyways I didnt want to message you. But Steve kept pressuring me to do so

The next day, Barbara sent another:

I feel so sorry for you. You are a disgusting pathetic human. You with these pathetic 8 followers who are so embarrassed to show their picture hah,hah,hah And you committed blaspheny when you said God laughed at me. I just got done praying and I heard no laughter. I am blessed with money, wealth and a wonderful husband and I'm healthy. You sound like a sick dog on your talk shows. Anyways I'm gonna talk to a mighty wind.

They are kind and act human and know the sick truth of you lol. Your soul will be rotting in Hell you disgusting creature.

Almighty Wind is a website run by a competing internet prophet whose followers make videos debunking Sherry's teachings. *A Mighty Wind* is a Christopher Guest film. Barbara meant the former, and it drove Sherry nuts. It wasn't that she feared being exposed by them so much as she hated whenever she had to acknowledge that she was powerless to stop the website's relentless mockery.

* * *

Steven asked Mike if he could use the audio from their conversation, or at least Mike's story in the anti-Sherry video he was planning. Mike was game, but hesitant.

"I have two things of concern for me, I guess," he told Steven in one of his recorded Facebook messages. "One would be any backlash because, like, 'Fuck off!' I don't need the issues, you know? I have a life to live. I'm happily married with two children. I don't need fucking constant e-mails and messages and texts of hate and anger.

"Secondly, I would like that, because I made a lot of friendships online with these people for a long, long time. I feel betrayed, and I feel I was done wrong and not just me, but my wife as well. And it hurt. It did."

Mike could already imagine how awful taking Sherry on would be. The threats, curses, and insults from people he knew, with whom he used to be friends. More than the threats, I think, was a looming understanding of what it means to have faith. Mike was thrown out. He didn't leave, and when you think about it, the only evidence he has against Sherry is she slandered his wife. He still believed in her power.

People say the strength of faith is doubt. It's not that you believe without question, but that your belief can endure questioning. The stakes are higher for people who believe in real demons on earth and the real possibility of being dragged to hell. It must be like living in a monster movie.

In the end, though, Mike wanted another say. If Steven could prove to others that Sherry was a fraud, if she could be discredited, Mike would be confident that he made the right choice. He said he was in, and he knew "Sherry's lemmings" would be out in force. They both had been a part of the mob and knew how relentless Sherry's warriors could be. Steven apologized for being one of the faces in the crowd at Mike's virtual stoning.

"I did it. I'm guilty of it," Mike said, shrugging off Steven's past. "Because of my anger towards Richard Brown over the years, when I heard that shit happened, I was telling everyone. I think I even messaged you about it. I tried to reach out to as many as I could because I was thinking, 'Oh fuck, man. I knew it all along! I knew this piece of shit! I knew! I knew!' But no. I didn't. I was just feeling an anger I was holding inside of me which is wrong, absolutely wrong. So, I apologized to Rich. Him and I are good now, man."

The idea that Brother Rich was alive tantalized Steven. He knew him as one of the old-school Shrinerites. Brother Rich had been to Sherry's house. He knew what she looked like, what she really was like. Steven believed that with Brother Rich's testimony on a big enough platform there was no reason they couldn't take Sherry down. Steven never understood that Sherry was invulnerable to the truth, and least of all the truth as presented by Steven Mineo. He changed his entire belief structure to one where Sherry was the final obstacle. Steven had no idea how wrong he was.

In the second before Sherry accused Barbara, Steven believed Richard Brown was dead and Kelly Pingilley was assassinated by NATO. These facts were proof the NWO was trying to bring Sherry down. Supporting her was the best way to fight them since Sherry was Lucifer's primary adversary. Steven believed that for years without question.

He had become part of a culture of static belief where new information is jammed into what he already believes or is discarded as false. If I believe something that I discover is wrongheaded or false, I can change my beliefs. Truthers gave up that ability (or had it taken from them, if you prefer). Many are too invested in the reality they inhabit to give it up. And both before and after Sherry, Steven inhabited a different reality.

Shrinerites believe they're living in *The Matrix*. Laying it out for me, MJ explained orgone warriors are the rebels, and The Bride are regular people living under Lucifer's sway. Demons can possess anyone at any time (just as Agent Smith could possess civilians in the movie) and use those bodies to attack the orgone warriors, leaving the husk of a slightly confused person when they unpossess them. That's one way Shrinerites identify spiritual attacks. If a person is aggressive or downright mean, they're just temporary pawns of Lucifer undergoing possession.

But Steven had leveled up, gone beyond Sherry's lies into a place that looked less like *The Matrix* and a lot more like *Invasion of the Body Snatchers*, where people were replaced by alien beings and you never knew who you were talking to. It wasn't just that Steven didn't know what was true anymore, he had no idea whom he could trust.

* * *

Steven spent nearly a week working on his first anti-Sherry YouTube video. He didn't seem to be planning a series at first, but after talking to Mike he knew he needed to talk to Brother Rich.

This first video would be the set-up. It would get people talking. The gist, according to Steven, was that Sherry Shriner was a false prophet surrounded by thugs who both financed her ministry and acted as her spiritual investigators and hitmen.

He called out Marianne and Jenna by name and, in what he thought of as a truth bomb, recounted his conversations with Beverly, who claimed he was among the 144,000 elect who would be taken to heaven with Sherry and the rest of the orgone warriors. Barbara even made a cameo defending herself, but they waited to publish it when it would have what Steven believed would be the maximum effect.

The last weekend in May came and went. Sherry must have figured Steven would go away after a while, like Nate Pingilley, Mike Hall, Richard Brown, and all the others. Sherry miscalculated. While she maintained her flock as well as her silence on the matter, Steven was hunched over his computer making videos. They were taken down after his death, but the titles remain: "SHERRY SHRINER SAID MY WIFE IS A REPTILIAN LOL! 14 YEARS I WAS A SUPPORTER OF SHERRY'S MINISTRY!"

He posted it on his blogger page May 29 at just about 7:30 p.m., just as Sherry's Monday night show was about to start. Then Steven and Barbara set about sharing it wherever they were able, posting the video on many of Sherry's followers' pages. Sherry was ignorant of this before her show, but there's no way she didn't know by the end.

When she discovered that Steven would not come slinking back nor would he fade away quietly, she prepared to release the hounds of hell upon him.

But Steven was a step ahead. While Sherry had been enjoying her weekend, Steven and Barbara had begun a quiet recruitment campaign, hunting down people whom Sherry had wronged or excommunicated, and building a coalition whose sole purpose was to expose Sherry Shriner. Steven intended to be relentless.

16

THANK GOD IT WASN'T THE REAL SHERRY THAT ACTUALLY BETRAYED ME.

"Did you have the courage to watch the whole video? Huh? Huh!?! Because I seen you and Barbara talking just now so I had to I had to speak on this." Steven's voice was getting louder in the Facebook audio message, straining to contain his anger. "You need to have the courage to watch the whole freakin' video!"

Steven's early exchanges are a window into the breadth of his anger. This one was with Cesar Macias. Cesar had reached out to Barbara, curious about all the rumors. Steven already had unfriended him, but when he saw Cesar might be an ally, Steven joined the conversation. He was certain there were people willing to hear negative things about Sherry and leave her ministry.

Steven continued, wound up now, talking as much to himself as to Cesar, sometimes screaming so loud his voice rumbles and breaks.

"I know it's hard, I know it's hard," he said, responding to a comment Cesar didn't make. This was a speech, not a conversation. "I've been supporting her for fourteen years! You realize how fucked up this is? What she did to us?"

Steven was in a rage now, and I felt for him. Sometimes you get so angry, so disgusted with whatever injustice you've endured that it swells in your chest and you can't stop or control your tone of voice and the louder you get, the more freely the rage flows. He turned on Barbara, insisting that she record a message telling Cesar what had been done to her and how fucked up it was.

"Tell him!" Steven was yelling again, and Barbara repeated what he had asked.

"It is very messed up what Sherry Shriner is doing to me," she said, sounding equal parts exasperated and afraid. Barbara's voice had a whiny, recalcitrant quality, as if she were resisting gravity. Barbara could be badgered into anything.

Cesar said he would watch the video, but Steven couldn't let it go.

"I hope The Most High puts you through this because you need to go through this. You need to wake up to what she really is!" Steven was trying to cool down now, knowing how he sounds when he starts yelling, but he came down too fast and his voice softened into a light, whiny half-sob. "You realize how much this is a mental bother? How much it mentally bothers us? I was suicidal, man, I thought of killing myself."

I imagine Steven sitting on the bed in his stale, oppressive little room crying while Barbara rubbed his back, his choking grief turning to sobs as his world came apart around him. It was going to be a long battle for all of them.

Later, Steven checked his YouTube counter, waiting for his truth bomb to go viral. It didn't. Even with all his messaging and promotion, Steven couldn't get the big views he desired.

"They're not even watching the video," he told Mike. "I had to disable the fucking, you know the, thumbs-up thing. It's like you could tell by their name they're not watching it."

His real anger came from his experience. Before, when someone made an anti-Sherry video, Steven led the rush to suppress it by adding negative comments and links to the "real truth" at SherryShriner.com. The irony in Truthers stamping out alternative takes is a thing of horrible beauty.

Steven knew he wouldn't get his video to catch fire with all the negative responses, and it stoked his fury. Why were these people so opposed to hearing the truth? Steven had seen firsthand that Sherry was a liar, that her claims to have spoken to Yah were false and that her claims against Barbara were false. The latter was the most critical for him.

Steven needed Sherry to recant or be stripped of her power. I think that was the only way he could know for sure that Barbara wasn't a reptilian. Steeped in Sherry's black-and-white world, Steven needed group proof and approval. He was a true believer in the democratization of information, and he was campaigning for his wife's humanity. That's why he spent his efforts trying to clear her name. Why else would he care what his turncoat comrades thought?

Steven was straddling two realities, and each of those seemed to be coming apart. He needed a unifying picture to hold onto, but the only one that was left was the one he had abandoned after the Twin Towers fell.

* * *

For years, Sherry had told wild tales about her clones, claiming the NWO had at least three clones made to replace her but hadn't gotten to her yet. There were mixed messages about how to deal with clones, and Shrinerites were under the impression that if you see your clone, you should kill it before it kills you, or you should run away. You can see how a story like that might appeal to the recently expelled Shrinerites.

Steven got a message from a woman called Karen whose daughter could speak to angels. She told Steven that she, too, had been cut off. Her crime was posting a picture of angels that offended Jenna.

"So after that Jenna unfriended me, and they removed me from Sherry's Orgone Warriors chat saying I'm a spy," Karen wrote. "They have hurt me many times so I was afraid to say anything."

She went on to explain that her daughter had seen orgone destroy demons, setting them aflame by proximity. The angels confirmed that orgone was real, so Karen had sent a bunch of money to Sherry to support her ministry. Karen's daughter also told her they attend a class God teaches every night and then fight demons and trolls until dawn when their spirits return to their bodies.

There is so much here. I don't have a guess at how old Karen's daughter is, but the fact that she orders her mother around via an ability to speak with angels disturbs me, more so if she's just a child. It made Steven a little uneasy, too. He didn't want to be the one to say how crazy she sounded, but Mike acknowledged the story's farfetchedness. Except the part where the psychic angel-whispering daughter said that Sherry was "not herself," that there were no angels around Sherry's house, and that a group of warriors would have to band together and find her. Steven actually chuckled his way through that line as he read it to Mike.

What's frustrating is they accepted this angel-whispering child's assertion that the real Sherry was gone, but decided everything else she said was fabricated. It is so hard to get a bead on their standards. It feels as if what they believe and why is case-specific, what they say is never bound by what they've said in the past.

Mike agreed that Sherry being replaced by a clone was the only reasonable way to explain her cutting off people who had been loyal supporters and evangelists. Sherry Shriner was dead, replaced by a clone. Mike needed to believe it. His voice was dreamy in the recording, as if he were giving a dying man's speech in a WWII movie, planning on eating that big steak when he got home. It solidified my impression of Mike as a good and honest guy who just got too turned around when the world couldn't provide him enough certainty.

"It would almost, like, give me a sense of relief, almost a little bit of vindication," Mike said, talking again about all the time and money she'd cost him. "Thank God it wasn't the real Sherry that actually betrayed me. It was some fuckin' whatever replacement, clone, hybrid. Who knows?"

"Wow," Steven said, listening to Mike's recording. And then to Barbara in the room, "He said he gave her a lot of money. Mike gave her a lot of money."

"Mike gave her money?" Barbara asked, incredulous.

"He did it for The Most High. We gave her money, too, hon," Steven said to a stunned silence. He backed off a bit, trying to make the statement less "we" and more "me," as if his donations were a thing of the distant past, something he had done before they met.

"Over the years," he said, qualifying. "I gave Sherry Shriner money. I'm about to sue this fucking bullfrog and get my money back!"

Steven added that he sent her money on GoFundMe and over PayPal (which maybe was where he kept his personal money), but it was a weird moment between two people without jobs talking about donations from the confines of a single room in a trailer. To her credit, Barbara seemed to send money to her kids, not to some internet preacher.

In July 2017, Sherry's GoFundMe was listed as having more than $125,000 in it. That's separate from her PayPal, not to mention all the mailed checks and cash.

* * *

With Barbara's expulsion and Steven's resignation, we lose our backstage pass to Sherry Shriner's private Facebook chat. When Sherry came off the air the night Steven posted his video, she must have returned to a chat room of tense people. People who had seen the video or knew of its existence and were waiting for instructions. While Sherry ranted about the Queen of England being a lizard and Trump's poorly constructed clone on her radio show that night, Steven and Barbara spread the word: Sherry Shriner was a false prophet.

That Steven thought he could win tells us so much about his ignorance and self-centeredness. At some level, he thought he mattered in the organization, that his support role was some sort of linchpin in Sherry's superstructure. Worse, he thought he cared about the truth, and having seen the light that others naturally would follow. But Steven wasn't a builder. He didn't offer an alternative to Sherry's theology. Steven was in the throes of a terminal temper tantrum, and like a disaffected babysitter, Sherry Shriner watched him struggle and rage with a detached amusement.

Still, Steven's video needed answering. Not point by point, but rather a different attack altogether. Seeing how outraged Steven was, and a little skeeved that Barbara had actually messaged her, Sherry continued to focus on Barbara. Barbara was such an easy target. She was spiritually promiscuous on Facebook, following whatever magic she fancied. She was friends with earth-based spiritualists Sherry considered witches. Best of all, it drove Steven nuts not to be able to defend his wife with any success.

Sherry took a screenshot of Barbara's post and reshared it for all her followers to see. Barbara's "food post" was itself a screen capture from Google images, not a meal she had eaten.

It took me about a minute to find it on a stock photo site. The dish looks to have been composed using ground beef from the grocery store rather than the hand-ground, trimmed sirloin restaurants tend to use. Made with raw beef and a raw egg, steak tartare can be dangerous if prepared with substandard ingredients. In the photo, the raw egg sits atop the very-red beef, almost glowing yellow contrasted with the visible chalaza (the stringy cord that attaches the yolk to the white). The preparation sits on a white plate with a white background, making the photo even less appealing. Diced onions, parsley, gherkins, and whole capers occupy the compass points on the dish.

Sherry took her people through the symbolism, cautioning them that Barbara was no low-level witch but rather a reptilian monster who craved blood in all its forms:

The hamburger dish contains elements of witchcraft North South East West.
The Egg (The Eye) is at the North.
South there are capers.
East there are herbs.
On the West, it's either Jalapenos or shit (they actually eat feces, they can it and call it beef bile).

This symbolism is supposed to be obvious, but I found it kind of impenetrable. The eye is meant to represent the Illuminati, I suppose, but nothing else besides the fact that she decided the gherkin relish was feces rings the occult bell for me. Again, it doesn't matter. It probably matters less to Sherry than it does to me. Her point, her goal, was to separate Barbara from the pack and make Steven choose. Once Steven decided to make a stand, she set her dogs on both of them.

And here's the thing: I do not know whether Barbara has ever eaten steak tartare. She claims to have and to have enjoyed it, but she seems as if she's caught between hanging onto the real point, which is that eating raw or bloody meat doesn't make you a Satanist, and assuring Steven that ingesting blood isn't her thing. This puts the talk she had with her son about it in context.

"Ok I just have one question How often did I eat raw meat????" she typed in a Facebook message. "Do you remember me eating raw meat alot?? What do you remember me eating alot?"

This is out of the blue after weeks without sending a Facebook message.

"I don't remember you eating raw meat a lot!" he responded. "Like really rare steaks and stuff!"

What an odd exchange. What a bizarre question to ask your son unless you were looking for some sort of verification, or your husband was. Barbara didn't need to prove to herself that she wasn't a witch—in the traditional sense, anyway. Moreover, she had eaten most every meal with Steven for the better part of a year. If she had, say, sent back a burger because it wasn't bloody enough, he would have noticed, if he cared. Still, it bothers me. Who was that question-and-answer session for? She had a similar exchange with her ex-husband, who remembered that she liked her steak rare but confirmed that she wasn't a reptilian before he disengaged.

It's worth saying that Barbara's Facebook contact with her children was sporadic, and the conversations leave me with the impression that they weren't talking much more (if at all) off Facebook. Her daughter didn't notice she was "married" until April or so. It still was February, right after they settled in as man and wife in the Poconos, the first time she reached out to her son as Barbara Mineo.

"Hello son. My husband steven sent you a request. He just wants to know my family. So I hope you accept," she wrote.

"Are you married?"

"lol not quite yet," she said. Then: "So let me know if you guys find that box with military stuff in it? Because I would love to get it."

They had contacted him because Steven wanted to get his hands on Barbara's old Army gear to add to his apocalypse stash. She seemed to send cash, birthday money, and a little boost now and then, but she asked her teenagers for a lot of advice as well. There was very little chit-chat online. It's not a criticism so much as it is an observation about a worldview based on self-alienation that I don't have a lot of access to.

In my world, the grown-ups are in charge of helping their kids come to terms with the world around them, not the other way around. Then again, I've never been in a position where I needed a third party to confirm I didn't eat raw meat and that I was not a reptilian.

As Steven and Barbara focused on their fight with Sherry Shriner, neither reached out to their families for support and guidance in any way that would compel anyone to intervene. They struggled to hold onto a life together that wasn't sustainable, that never could have been. If they sought help, they sought it on their own terms and as part of the war to dethrone the prophet.

I'm reminded of how Kelly's friends and family reacted to her beliefs before and after her suicide. Kelly was in a position where she already had, of her own accord, made conversation about Sherry Shriner's legitimacy a nonstarter.

I imagine it was the same for Steven, except he had the added bonus of feeling responsible for Barbara as her husband and pro-tector. At every turn, I feel like I want to grab him and say, "You're well shed of Sherry Shriner. Just walk away." But Steven wasn't just a true believer, which made leaving hard enough, he also was offended by the inequity.

On one hand, Steven had his crumbling realities. On the other, he was mad that someone was lying about him. He wanted closure, I think, almost as much as he wanted Sherry exposed. Almost. I don't think it's unreasonable to say that, in the end,

Steven was consumed by his need for revenge and his failure to get it.

The problem was Steven was going to war with a fiction. Sherry Shriner wasn't much more real than Lucifer or any other of the metaphysical beings he fought. Steven was at war with a Sherry who existed only on the internet. Sure, there was a person typing who also was named Sherry Shriner, but the persona wasn't the person. Sherry Shriner the person was pitiable, drowning in the backwoods life of mediocrity she had tried to escape. Queen Shazurazy was a lot more like a malevolent god, setting the scampering beings below her to fight for her amusement and to quake at her power.

Steven couldn't ever have defeated that because it wasn't, isn't, real. Her power was as manufactured as her fairy tales about meeting God and the devil in heaven or the constant failed attacks on her spirit and person by the US government. Sherry had been a professional prophet for too long for Steven to undermine her.

* * *

If we're going to talk about witches, unfortunately we're going to have to talk about ritual excrement feasts. Barbara Rogers wasn't the only person Sherry ever accused of eating feces. For her, it was part of the larger NWO culture. This is a world where the shadow government runs a child sex-slavery ring. Where celebrities have orgies in the blood of children to exalt their evil master and prove their fealty. All Truthers believe a version of this.

Sherry had for years claimed to have proof that these blood orgies included feces-eating rituals. As she was promoting her books and ministry in the summer of 2016, Sherry was invited on *The Truth Train with Liberty Lisa*, a BlogTalkRadio show.

Lisa was fascinated by Sherry's blood and feces stories. I spoke with her at length and found her charming and noncombative. Lisa was a media professional. She conducted interviews with genuine interest and engagement. Lisa tried to be gracious with her guests even, and maybe especially, when they didn't see eye to eye. When we spoke, she acknowledged and accepted that I wasn't on her wavelength and had no interest in it besides trying to find a better understanding of the Christian Truther culture.

Lisa had approached Sherry because she thought Sherry had some good information about the blood-and-feces-eating rituals that were incorporated into the pedophile orgies organized by the government and the Hollywood elites. The Jeffrey Epstein story had just broken when I spoke with her. The Epstein story confirmed for the entire Truther community that Senator Hillary Clinton was running a child sex-slavery ring all along.

Throughout her ministry, Sherry turned to feces-eating as a topic more often than seemed necessary, but maybe it's just my weak stomach. It is a claim that isn't as specific to her as, say, orgone, but Sherry's claim of proof made her attractive as a potential guest. Lisa wouldn't learn that Sherry was fabricating the whole story until her show spun off the rails.

As Lisa finished her introduction and brought Sherry on air, I heard the telltale hum of Sherry's cheap internet connection. The one that heralded her voice in each of her own radio shows. Sherry provided her bona fides and launched into why God shared with her His revealed truth about the alien agenda, reptilians, and the NWO plan for world domination. She elaborated about orgone's power, and what it was like to interview Lucifer while God held him captive in heaven.

Lisa was dumbstruck. You can hear her hesitation as Sherry ranted and rambled—a good hostess who was deciding how to ask her guest to stop shitting on the living room rug.

By the fifteen-minute mark or so, after several attempts to get the interview back on track, Lisa went to the phones. The first caller was Beverly Nelson, who annotated Sherry's rant, praising her as the Daughter of The Most High and extolling the power of orgone.

Lisa stuttered a thanks. She was half-outraged, half-shocked at the insanity coming from Sherry and the absolute disregard for the cultural norms of being interviewed. The second caller provided some backup, going on the attack against Sherry and her orgone.

What Sherry and much of the Christian Truther movement have in common is a hatred of idolatry that very well may date back to the old world, but certainly was entrenched as part of the American Baptist anti-Catholic sentiment. Sherry left the Baptist church of her youth after concluding they were phonies who lacked spiritual understanding. But those early beliefs left their imprint. Baptists I've spoken to genuinely believe that Catholics are idol worshippers. Where I live in rural America many don't know Catholicism is a Christian denomination, let alone one of the oldest.

As mainstream religion continues to bleed market share, there's been a weird shift with (let's call them) liberal Baptists accepting that maybe the idolatry thing is a bit overdone with Catholics, and conservative Baptists openly considering them Satan worshippers. It's a trend we continue to ignore at our own peril, and certainly why the Christian Truther movement has legs.

In the struggle to hang onto old-time religion, people are much more interested in hellfire, the devil's presence in the world, and reconciling those facts with the scientific and technological breakthroughs of the last one hundred years.

Lisa's caller, like many of Sherry's detractors from outside the cult, accused the Shrinerites of worshiping rocks. Sherry tried to explain about Wilhelm Reich and how God told her about orgone, but she didn't make much headway. From there conversation devolved into arguments about doctrine and dogma as it involved what aliens really were. For traditional Christians aliens were demons, while for Sherry they were Lucifer's generals, superior to and more dangerous than any demon could be.

Listening three years after that show, it was nice to hear Sherry outshouted for a change. It was also an insight into how thin-skinned she really was. When speaking with someone subservient, Sherry was a firecracker, but when pressed, she cracked. Eventually Sherry rang off, retreating to the comfort and safety of people who were afraid not to worship her. Of course, she sent her minions after Lisa. In addition to death threats and other vile real-world communications, Lisa said she was spiritually attacked for two weeks.

I had been laboring under the misapprehension that spiritual warfare was confined to good people attacking evil ones with prayer and orgone, asking God to intercede on their behalf. Lisa cleared that up for me. She explained that spiritual attacks can be launched by evil people against good people as well. I guess it makes sense. It's called spiritual warfare after all, but I asked her to explain how one knows whether they're being spiritually attacked.

"It'd be kind of like a dark presence upon entering a room, and you can literally feel it. Just the feeling of being targeted and spied on. One part of it is also nightmares," she said. "During that time, I remember having nightmares and just a feeling of uneasiness. Sometimes you'll get manifestations, sometimes you might have weird things happen, like something just randomly falling off of a table."

Having never been the recipient of hate mail and death threats myself, I thought the legitimate anxiety of the experience could cause most of that, except for the part about things falling off tables, but Lisa was emphatic. She hosts a fringe radio show in the bowels of the internet where the trolls go to sharpen their knives. Hate mail and death threats are common currency down there, and she was no stranger to them. She insisted that what happened after her confrontation with Sherry was more than the usual trolling.

That stuck with me, partly because I believed her and partly because I used her legitimate belief to project myself further into this strange world where spiritual attacks were real.

When I was a kid, I had an aunt who could conjure St. Anthony, patron saint of, among other things, lost objects. Once we had searched exhaustively, sometimes for days, we would call her and ask her to pray. It was a last resort only, because you didn't want to pester her or St. Anthony. But once you called Aunt Pat, it was a given that the object would turn up. We didn't even think of it as prayer or intercession so much as magic.

I think a lot of us have stories about psychic relatives we don't believe in and still listen to, but there are people whose entire lives are laser-focused on the supernatural. For them, anxiety, depression, and even post-traumatic stress are demonic infections or possession. We can laugh and say that it's a primitive throwback to "the humors" the Greeks used to diagnose things they couldn't understand, but it misses the point. If a person believes that they are being attacked by devils in a meaningful and literal sense, that's how they're going to respond.

I lost my class ring in the snow. I called Aunt Pat and got it back. Lisa was beset by negative spiritual energy, and she prayed her way out of it. She no more thought of dealing with the spiritual attacks as if they were anxiety than I thought about just looking harder or longer for that ring. And as long as there are no obvious ill effects, there's no point questioning the practice.

Unfortunately, there are ill effects that come from inhabiting a complete fiction all the time. There develops a gap in reality that widens the longer it's open, until the yaw is such that it isn't worth the effort or the danger to cross. If prayer is your only defense against deepening depression and anxiety, things can go terribly wrong. We see it all the time. We're seeing it now as people cling to the surety of conspiracy theory rather than face the gray world of choice and consequence.

For Lisa, there was no doubt that Sherry was running a cult, but that it was much more like a satanic cult than anyone on the inside even realized. Lisa tended to believe that Paul the Apostle was a legitimate Christian commentator and was repulsed by the idea that Sherry discounted it all as the work of the devil. For Lisa, discounting such a significant portion of the Bible was concerning, but the orgone worship was the kicker.

17

I'M NOT SURE ALL THE MONEY WAS GOING TOWARD ORGONE.

The Richard Brown Interviews. That's what a few of us who have been digging into this part of Steven's life have come to call them with the reverence of Bigfoot hunters. Everyone seems sure they must be somewhere because, after all, everything deleted from YouTube is somewhere. I was not able to track them down.

There were quotes from the interviews in early reporting on Steven's death, and many of them coincide with Steven and Richard's recorded Facebook Messenger conversations. Those conversations trace a torrid bromance over the course of a little more than two weeks in June 2017.

We all like to feel important, and Brother Rich hadn't had much of a profile after his exile. I don't think he craved the attention so much as the authority tied up with being among Sherry Shriner's top go-to people. Like a speechwriter, maybe, happier to be able to affect what an audience hears without having to get them to listen.

It's one of the things Mike Hall disliked about him. Richard had a tendency to comment on Sherry's work in a way that praised and annotated. Mike said it bothered him that "all the girls" called him Brother Rich. At the time, he thought Brother Rich was making being an orgone warrior about putting Sherry on a pedestal, and Mike wasn't wrong.

Brother Rich guested on Johnny Galvan's *The Everything Full-Fledged Reality Show* in April 2015. That interview, which we do still have, gives a peek into Brother Rich at the height of his importance to Sherry Shriner. When Brother Rich talks, it is to educate, and it comes through in his voice, every fact delivered with a tone that suggested he was a little embarrassed to state the obvious. Galvan was a super fan greedy to talk to an insider: What was Sherry really like to be around? What did Sherry look like? How did she dress? What did she eat? Self-assured and more than a little condescending, Brother Rich knew he was one of the few people who had visited Sherry Shriner's home, but he deflected questions about the prophet's private life.

Sherry was listening that night, and she encouraged her followers to do the same. She must have beamed when Brother Rich talked about how spaceships hovered over Sherry's house testing for weaknesses in her orgone defenses. He and Sherry would sit out in her driveway for hours watching what most people mistook for shooting stars but, in reality, were spaceships exploding after contact with the orgone-saturated atmosphere above Sherry's home.

Sherry's power came from confirmations like this. Her claims about being under siege took on so much more weight with independent verification. The salient story was about being present for a government attack on Sherry's home. Brother Rich had been there for dinner and must have been hit by an energy ray intended for Sherry. His guts twisted in agony, and Brother Rich started shitting black bile. He recovered, he told Johnny, but it was a mere glimpse into what Sherry goes through. Attacks on her health were legendary, and Brother Rich was there to confirm they were legitimate.

That was the orgone warrior's lot. Johnny hung on every word.

If he hadn't betrayed Kelly Pingilley, Brother Rich might be a tragic figure in a superhero movie—the henchman who realizes too late he is working for evil and sacrifices himself to save the heroes. I think he sees himself that way. Where many questioned Sherry's teachings, Brother Rich never did. He told Mike he went to her as a friend, worried that as her ministry became more lucrative, she might have been making it too much about her and not enough about God. For perspective, this is a guy who referred to her as Prophet of The Most High and Yah's Ambassador on Earth. Daughter of The Most High seemed like a stretch, though, as did Queen of Heaven.

Richard Brown knew how to take Sherry down, but Brother Rich was going to need to be convinced before he tried again. Setting aside the two false deaths she had attributed to him, Brother Rich remembered the harassment and the utter rejection from people who weren't only his friends, but who had respected him as a biblical and Sherry Shriner authority. Now he was all on his own, his wife was sick with cancer, and the last thing he needed was to get in another tangle with Sherry Shriner.

When Steven messaged and asked if he would help make a video discrediting Sherry, the former Shrinerite was interested but aloof. Throughout his involvement, Brother Rich participated on his own terms. He knew that he was the expert and expected deference. Steven, for whom deference hadn't worked out so well, didn't push back too hard. He needed the man's authority. Brother Rich teased that he had information about Sherry that would drive all her followers away. Steven needed that information.

* * *

Steven drew first blood with his May 29 video, and his opponent returned fire with her public call to arms against him and Barbara on May 30 by reposting the cut-and-pasted steak tartare post with her symbolism commentary.

I think Steven's post got more attention than she expected, but Sherry was confident she had it handled. Marianne was posting Sherry videos on both Steven's Facebook page and on YouTube. Sherry herself took the time to go on and comment (although Steven said he refused to read it). Steven's frustration came less from the attacks against his video than from the fact that no one was watching it. Comments like this one from Shelly Long drove him over the edge:

> Steve, listen. I'm trying to make a point. Whether your wife is or is not a which, military plant, reptilian, or whatever the case derogatory or negative, why would you feel the need to post a video on YouTube to discredit and destroy Sherry and all of the work that she has done for over a decade because she said something that you didn't agree with? I'm sorry if you and your wife's feelings are hurt, but whether or not they are true is irrelevant. What is relevant is the fact that all of us have listened to Sherry for the last decade and everything else she has said has been true. Why would you feel the need to have to publicly destroy her because she held an opinion about your wife that you didn't agree with?

To this and other posts like them, all Steven could write was, "Did you watch the whole video? It is not just me she is doing this to! This video gives a lot of sad truth about Sherry Shriner."

Barbara brought up Kelly Pingilley, as did others. Steven teased the "Rick card" referencing the true story about Brother Rich, which must have made Sherry sweat a bit.

Steven confided to Mike that Barbara was running out of gas on the whole revenge trip, which makes utter sense. Why would she need her name cleared among internet trolls and reptilian conspiracists? These weren't her friends, they were Steven's. She didn't really care except that the attacks against her were driving Steven mad. Her husband was struggling, and Barbara was unequipped for it.

Paying the bills, going to bars, staying up late, messing around on the internet. Millions of people live their entire adult lives like this without consequence, but also without having relationships that can stand up to crises. Sturdy adult relationships require mutual responsibility for the other's mental or emotional well-being; otherwise, they crumble.

Adult relationships are boring, difficult, and not the reason anyone chooses the kind of life that Barbara and Steven had. When Steven spoke with Mike about Barbara, you got the idea Steven was on borrowed time with her. He knew he was leaning too hard on a woman who didn't want to be leaned on at all.

"Every now and then I am breaking down a little bit. I'm trying not to let that happen. I've started to become concerned for my wife because she's kind of like saying she's gotta get through this too," he said. His voice quiet, confessional. "She's tougher when it comes to all this. She's more stronger than me, and I just hope she doesn't give up on me. I don't think she's going to. I just gotta be stronger. She won't, I just, she's, she's just gotta see me stronger." The last bit was directed at himself as much as at Mike. A quiet resolution.

Barbara liked the idea that Steven was young and aggressive, that he was into anime and the supernatural, but she hadn't signed up to spend all her time consoling a sobbing man-child who lost his make-believe friends.

Barbara started having Steven take some of the meds she had been prescribed for her bipolar disorder. There wasn't anything recreational about them. Barbara was on a host of drugs. We don't know which of Barbara's other prescriptions, if any, Steven took over the course of his breakdown, but he at least took her Prozac. I'm sure she felt Steven needed something to help level him out. Barbara was a mother of convenience, doing the best she could to help Steven's hurt go away, even if it meant embracing his pointless crusade.

* * *

Barbara had a difficult message to write. She deleted all of her "witchy" Facebook friends after the Shrinerites accused her, and there were a number. *Witch* is an antiquated and sometimes derisive term that some alternative spiritual practitioners embrace and others shun. The few I know are more the Earth-worshiping hippie types than of the black hat and broomstick variety, but for the Shrinerites there is only one type of witch. Theirs is a simple world divided into the saved and passive or active Satan worshippers.

Rather than try to explain her relationship with questionable people to Steven, Barbara deleted them. But as Steven continued prosecuting his war, he needed more allies, and he encouraged her to start reaching out to her witch friends to help spread his anti-Sherry rhetoric.

The most famous witch on Barbara's list was Sarah R. Adams. Sarah doesn't describe herself as a witch. Her official web page describes her as an intuitive healer who uses herbs, essential oils, and homeopathy to treat ailments. She'd been featured on Gaia TV. Sarah is an attractive, bronze, full-lipped woman who radiates more a comfort with her body than overt sexuality. She couldn't be much more different from Sherry Shriner.

In the few videos I've watched, she's charming and comfortable in conversation, and even though the conversations are about the mystical, she doesn't radiate the kind of crazy you might expect. It's someplace between fringe and delusional, but never malicious. Or maybe my bar is just way too low now. Sarah's Facebook page has the same kinds of posts as Sherry's, they're just less mean. Sure, the Illuminati are still running everything, and, yes, people are sometimes possessed, and, of course, evil forces are everywhere, but given all that, try and find inner peace where you can.

Barbara liked following Sarah, whose Facebook page was a combination of positive affirmations and self-care tips and tricks couched in the metaphysical. Sarah talks to angels and practices magic, but appears to focus too much on the individual to ever lead a cult. She's more a lifestyle guru. Once Steven encouraged Barbara to reconnect with Sarah, she opened with an apology message. In it, she said she was forced to delete Sarah as a friend and recounted the accusations made against her and Steven. Barbara also wanted to send along information about Sherry Shriner who claimed that Sarah was a walking dimensional port-hole through whom Lilith, an agent of Satan and Adam's first wife (it's a long story), speaks.

Sarah thanked her and admonished Barbara about making better dietary choices when it came to eating red meat. Then she said Sherry wasn't the only cult leader on her radar. Sarah told Barbara she'd been running into a lot of them lately, adding that she might sue Sherry for the attack, but she sent her a takedown notice instead.

"I told her to grow up and use her time to do better than stalk me and harm the very people who follow her," Sarah told Barbara, who then asked her opinion of Sherry Shriner.

"I think she is being used by lower forces. She is deceived, she is using the energy of her following for things less than noble," Sarah said, "She treated you and your husband bad, this shows her true colors."

Barbara agreed, telling Sarah that Sherry had called her a witch, a reptilian sleeper cell, and a vampire.

"Her own reflection. She is trying to project her own essence onto you," Sarah said. She went on to explain to Barbara that Sherry was possessed before suggesting that Sherry hid her face because she was embarrassed by the way she looks.

The two had run in the same prophet circles for a while, and Barbara thought they had been friends. Sarah let the observation pass, allowing only that she would never be friends with someone who abuses people. Barbara decided to ask a pointed question: "Do you think Sherry Shriner is a liar?"

And Sarah did not dissemble on this.

"Yes I think she is and I wish not to speak about her more," she said. "She must attack the target and make them look bad. She is using abuser tactics."

I think this is the part where Barbara was supposed to ask Sarah to help promote Steven's newest video, featuring Brother Rich, but the opportunity must have passed because she signed off without comment.

Barbara relayed Sarah's insights. Sherry Shriner was either possessed or just a petty, abusive person unworthy of people's trust. And let's be clear, if it was negative information about Sherry Shriner, then it was true for Steven. Reviewing his research process in retrospect is like watching a child fill an Easter basket with hand grenades. When he believed in Sherry Shriner, his facts had context. Now there were too many things to believe, too much contradictory information to process as a flood of new allegations flowed without obstacle into his conspiracy brain and were incorporated into a single, cacophonous drone.

Sherry was abusive.

Sherry was possessed.

Sherry was a clone.

Sherry was a lizard.

Sherry was programmed.

In Steven's last weeks, he believed all of this and more. Steven collected facts about Sherry Shriner, but not a story. He didn't have the wherewithal to sort all the information. Sometimes when Brother Rich said something complicated, Steven repeated it back, testing out the words to hear how they sounded coming out of his mouth. As with so many other Truthers, he internalized ideas without understanding—he was content that knowing the truth was the same as understanding it. This is fine when the truth is easy, like "Thou Shalt Not Steal." It gets more complicated when it comes to things like particle physics.

* * *

When Sherry began incorporating the Mandela Effect into her show, it captured Steven's imagination in a big way. He made videos looking into it and found "real-world" examples all the time. The last was just a week before his death.

The Mandela Effect is a shared false memory phenomenon, coined by paranormal researcher Fiona Broome in 2010. Apparently, a number of people believed Nelson Mandela died in prison in 1983. They all had clear memories of it happening, even though Mandela was released in 1990, served as president of South Africa for five years, and did not die until 2013. It's possible that these were people who just didn't pay attention to international politics, but that sounds a lot like an official explanation. Once the shared false memory effect had a name, people had a ready explanation why memories differ: multiple timelines. That notion sprouts from the "multiple universes" interpretation of quantum physics.

Sherry's people lived in awe of CERN, the European Organization for Nuclear Research, home to the Large Hadron Collider and birthplace of the internet, and they weren't alone. What goes on there in Switzerland is secret, theoretical, and beyond the scope of ordinary people's intellects. As Steven put it, "The technology that we use on a daily basis is amazing and used to be in Sci-Fi movies, but can you imagine the high-tech stuff that the powers-that-be are hiding from the public?"

Once the conspiracy crowd caught onto the theoretical existence of multiple timelines and time travel, there was no end to the supernatural applications. Take, for example, quantum suicide. It's a variation of Schrodinger's cat, which was a thought experiment designed to show people were thinking about quantum physics the wrong way. Schrodinger had a problem with prevailing quantum physics theories of the day, which implied that, depending upon how you measured particles, a cat in a box could be alive and dead at the same time. Since this wasn't possible, the theories were flawed. What many of us know about Schrodinger's cat is that it proved, via quantum physics, that there are multiple realities. We know this because it's the most fun way to think about it, not because it's true.

Quantum suicide is the same thing, designed to further prove how little we understand quantum physics, and it has spawned the same result, "proof" that there are multiple timelines. The difference is *you* are in the box instead of the cat. Depending upon how you measure the particles, when you put a gun to your head and pull the trigger, it either goes off or it doesn't. Combine this with the Mandela Effect and you introduce the reason for multiple timelines. Sometimes you have a near-death experience. Sometimes you die. And sometimes you have a near-death experience and remember dying.

Those are the instances where one of your timelines ended, but you continued on in an alternate reality where everything is a little different. People are meaner to you, they don't recall things you remember, and remember things that you don't.

The Large Hadron Collider and CERN made their way onto Sherry's shows as early as 2010. CERN had announced it would try to re-create a Big Bang, which thrilled and terrified Sherry's listeners. From then on, CERN was on Steven's radar. It spiked again the next year when Sherry said she wasn't sure whether or not CERN was behind the Mandela Effect, but by mid-2016, they were linked in Steven's understanding about time travel and the nature of multiple realities.

During the last few weeks of his life, Steven shared a story about the Statue of Liberty. Many people say they remember going up in the arm to the torch, but the arm has been off-limits since the 1916 "Black Tom" explosion. One of the largest man-made non-nuclear explosions in history was the work of saboteurs, if you believe the official story, although with a terrorist plot this size you can never be sure what happened. Some still claim it was an accident. The explosion accomplished two things: the closing of the Statue of Liberty arm, and the establishment of an American domestic security apparatus.

Steven shared a post about it, saying lots of people swear they remember being up in the arm of the Statue of Liberty, which is an example of the Mandela Effect proving an alternate reality.

"I watched this one video where this guy discovered his car had turned from red to white and he was shocked," a friend responded. "He calls his friends and they are like, 'What is wrong with you? It has always been white … [the guy replied] That was one of the biggest reasons I chose that car, for the color!' I feel we may see more and more people sharing personal crazy changes in their personal lives."

"I completely agree," Steven said. "When these things start hitting people personally, I believe that's when most people will start waking up to this phenomena."

Steven claimed to have already experienced the Mandela Effect. Bragg Organic Vinegar used to be Bragg's, he remembered it distinctly. In fact, on the label there was a description that said, Bragg's organic vinegar. Steven explained that this is called reality residue from the former reality (in fact, it was just the company using its name in the possessive). He says former, not alternate, indicating that one reality has passed and another one continues.

It must've comforted him, the idea that there was another reality where this didn't happen. That at any moment, his life on this rotten timeline would end, and he would continue on in another (better) reality. A reality where Sherry wasn't a liar, and you could walk right up to Liberty's torch and take in New York City, feel the crisp air, and know that all was right in the world. It would be absolute heaven.

* * *

There is little doubt that the Shrinerites register reality in a way many of the rest of us just don't. It's hard to come to terms with their reality because their interpretations of events seem too made up to be real beliefs, and that's tough to get past. I was captivated by the naked honesty with which Brother Rich, Steven, and Mike spoke about monsters and demons in their everyday lives.

For example, Brother Rich claimed black helicopters and field agents kept tabs on him. He claimed on multiple occasions that he saw them all the time. Brother Rich also claimed that his brother-in-law (Richard said the guy was an FBI agent) warned him not to expose too much about them. "Keep flying under the radar," the brother-in-law told him.

I like this story because it could very well be true. Tone is everything, and if your brother-in-law is telling people helicopters are following them, it makes perfect sense to warn them not to talk about it too much. What's tantalizing, though, is supposing that the brother-in-law is not FBI, but lied to get Brother Rich to cool out about his pursuers.

In a story with no rules, anything is possible, but whenever a Shrinerite tells a story about someone from outside the cult, I have to wonder whether that person is only humoring them. For people outside of the cult, it's the only way to keep a relationship with someone inside. It makes me wonder how much Barbara was humoring Steven.

Brother Rich had been expelled from Sherry's court more than a year before, then Mike was ousted, and now Steven. As the three conferred, they reinforced one another's conjectures using their well-honed conspiracy skills to reinterpret what they used to say they believed.

With the distance of time, Brother Rich had been able to put some of his experiences with Sherry into perspective.

"She had a whole garage for making orgone," Brother Rich said. "She had a huge operation for making it, but I believe she also made dead orgone from some of the pucks and blasters I saw."

No one asked why Brother Rich did nothing at the time, why he let Sherry send out negative orgone. They couldn't. Brother Rich wasn't the one on trial here.

"When I was at her house, I knew something evil was there," Richard said. "After we ate dinner, my insides got nuked from a microwave weapon, everything I defecated came out as black liquid."

It's almost identical to the story he told Johnny Galvan, when he was trying to prove Sherry was Lucifer's mortal enemy. The story is the same, but the interpretation is different. A congenital, infuriating disregard for things they've said and done made this story that much harder to write and follow.

It isn't just Sherry, it's all of them. I think the general attraction is blame without responsibility. Beyond the reticence to do the kind of research historians or trained theologians do, there's this belief that ignoring what you did or said wrong is the same as undoing it. Conspiracy theorists point and point and point with the aim, I believe, of staying ahead of the lies they tell themselves.

When it came to Sherry having been replaced, the more they thought about it, the more sense it made. Why would Sherry embark on a program against her most potent, powerful orgone warriors unless it was part of a larger plan to undermine the earth's defenses she claimed to be establishing?

Brother Rich was convinced. As he saw it, the new Sherry was making bad orgone. The new Sherry poisoned him with an energy ray. The new Sherry was in it for the money rather than for the glory of The Most High.

"She probably felt that she was getting close to being busted because I'm not sure all the money was going toward orgone," Brother Rich told them. "Her husband wasn't working so you know she had to pay the bills."

Richard was rolling now: "You remember Ann Cooper? Do you remember Michelle and Jim from Pennsylvania who she kicked to the curb? They said she wasn't doing what father felt that he wanted her to do. She's a con artist playing with those who lost hope in mainstream religion and government."

Richard said Beverly sent a big chunk of her husband's paycheck to Sherry. I suspect, for many, donating to Sherry became a cost they justified by continuing to pay. Steven would never comprehend that Sherry's followers were too invested for him to convert. And it wasn't as if he claimed he would be a better leader, or that Sherry was wrong or even a thief. Steven was mad at her, so he called her a false prophet. That might be Sherry's greatest gift. No one said she was a dowdy, middle-aged woman trolling the internet with lies. They said she was either a prophet from God or from Satan. She had a built-in mysticism that felt impossible to explain.

Sherry denied she ran a cult, and from a naive standpoint it's true. Her followers didn't live on her compound. They came and went as they pleased, and there was no rigorous reprogramming routine. What Sherry did was less reprogramming than hacking. She directed people's paranoia, gave it focus, and people reprogrammed themselves.

Throughout this entire inquiry I struggled with Sherry's power, but watching her hordes and the excommunicated do battle over her word, it occurred to me that Sherry's power didn't rest with her. It rested in her followers' commitment to self-deception. She provided the template, and her followers just filled it in themselves. They already felt persecuted and marginalized—abused and abandoned by religious and secular leaders—and Sherry gave them permission to feel persecuted. She confirmed their worst fears, and they appreciated her honesty. When she told them she had been attacked, they believed her because it made their own hard lives the result of demonic intervention. As long as they followed Sherry, nothing they said or did could be held against them.

Steven believed in witches, vampires, super soldiers, and the like. He couldn't bring himself to claim that Sherry was wrong about their existence any more than he could accept that the world wasn't on the brink of economic collapse and martial law. Everything she taught was part of who Steven was. It was part of who he was before he ever discovered Sherry Shriner; she just gave him a focal point.

That Sherry was just a fraudster never even made the list of top reasons she had taken people's money and their help and then discarded them. When she first accused Barbara, Steven wondered whether maybe Sherry was just making it all up as she went along, and his mind rejected it. Given that she couldn't be a fraud, there had to be another explanation. A more sinister one.

Steven, Mike, and Brother Rich debated whether Sherry had died and been replaced by a clone, and settled on that as the most reasonable explanation. In their reality, someone you trust doesn't cheat you unless they've been replaced or possessed. Why would it be different for that reality's architect?

Once, not too long before Sherry banned him, Richard visited the Shriner home. Sherry told him that the Ark of the Covenant, the golden box said to house the original Ten Commandments, as portrayed in the Indiana Jones movies, was buried in her backyard. She was mad that he wouldn't believe her.

Hearing this story was the first time it occurred to me that Sherry maybe wanted to see how many lies a person can endure before they snap. Try and put yourself in a position where you could confidently, and without even the slightest smirk, turn to another grown-up and tell them the Ark is buried in your backyard. Further imagine getting enraged when they don't believe you. From there, try and conceive why you would do such a thing.

We all know people who will make outrageous claim upon outrageous claim until they're called on it. But what if that person has the power to eliminate any voices of dissent no matter how improbable the claim? Where does it end?

This is the audacity that made Sherry Shriner such an effective cult leader. She not only had a deep and abiding contempt for the truth, but also for her followers. There was no base or nonsensical claim she could make that would drive them away. If anyone raised a complaint, they were summarily dismissed and driven out, attacked on their personal web pages, text messages, email accounts, and social media. There was a price to pay for failing to submit to Sherry. It's just that from the outside it seemed too trivial.

Maybe Sherry didn't have a commune to expel dissenters from, but she had something better. Sherry Shriner had her own reality, and once you were banned from that, you had better pray you have another reality to embrace.

Steven Mineo spent so much time in Sherry's world that he couldn't imagine anything happening outside of it, which is why he was so desperate to discredit her. Steven didn't want to be back under Sherry's power so much as back into the reality she created. So he resumed attacking her teachings in his effort to prove she was a false prophet.

* * *

Steven released his second anti-Sherry YouTube video on June 2. Titled, "Interview with Richard Brown He Was One of Sherry Shriner's Hardcore Supporters," Steven thought the film was proof that Brother Richard was not dead or in hell, but rather making orgone as he always had.

"If I was a clone, or if I was in Hell, why is it that I made a video about orgone all around me? I've got tons of orgone all around me," Brother Rich was reported to have said in part of the video. "She lied and said I told her to get rid of her orgone. I never said that. I actually went to her house and rebuilt her orgone stonehedge."

Richard Brown reposted the video on Steven's timeline, saying, "Now we'll let Father take it from here," a kind of meta-physical mic drop. Even though the video wasn't the viral hit Steven wanted it to be, he succeeded in posting something that got to Sherry in a meaningful way. Brother Rich coming out was a huge deal. Marianne Mulloy nearly lost her mind. She spammed the post with a few Sherry Shriner videos and went on to debunk Richard Brown's existence to his face:

> The black Richard Brown (not his real name) died on March 22nd, 2016. Rich was trash talking Sherry to some of his coworkers. Yahuah had enough. Rich was dead before he hit the floor. Rich is a resident of hell. So is his FBI handler. (Doug White another fbi troll notice the color as a name showed up on one of Sherry's orgone missions with what looked like Kristy Hall who looked really pissed. Winds were blowing at 60mph and she was dressed in a little jogging outfit. LOL) Maybe y'all like burning in a lake of fire for eternity. But prior to your death you can still repent.

The video didn't make a lick of difference. What's more interesting here, though, is that once the Richard Brown video dropped, the Shrinerites pretended not to notice. Today he is forgotten among them, part of an erased reality, not even dead and in hell. In the immediate aftermath, though, the Shrinerites responded as expected.

One of Sherry's tenets was that clones don't know they're clones any more than possessed people know they're possessed. Sherry knew Richard was alive, but I suspect Marianne truly believed at this point that Steven was in league with the devil. Hell, Steven and his allies believed that Sherry had been replaced and none of her friends or family knew it. This is a world where "it was probably a clone" is a legitimate response.

Mike had started a Facebook group chat called Curbside Warriors for the anticipated flood of Sherry's former followers to find refuge. He didn't have any takers. Steven, Brother Rich, Barbara, and the few others made up the meager resistance.

Steven believed that having Brother Rich talk about his personal experiences with Sherry would deal the biggest blow. According to the former Shrinerite, Sherry Shriner was a smoker, and she ate and liked shellfish (which were just as prohibited as bloody meat in the Bible). Plus, and Steven gravitated toward this,

Sherry was obese. He thought once Brother Rich showed everyone else that Sherry was so base, she would lose her authority over them.

It is possible that Brother Rich was just too much of a gentleman to make videos calling out Sherry for eating shrimp, smoking, and being overweight. What might make more sense, though, is that Brother Rich broke the prohibitions right along with her. Either way, the more insistent Steven was about an ad hominem attack, the more Brother Rich resisted.

Brother Rich encouraged Steven to take Sherry down "the way the Lord wants." That meant revealing the errors in her teachings rather than in her personal life. For Richard, Sherry was stealing pagan traditions and ideals to repurpose as her own theology. If you're not at all familiar with the history of religion, the abridged version is many religions have similar stories and myths. From the story of the flood to Christ's resurrection, the Christian narratives are similar to much more ancient stories. There's nothing nefarious about this. We fall into the stories we know. Popular stories are natural reference points for telling new ones.

In addition to claiming to be the Queen of Heaven, Sherry sometimes called herself Queen of Fire. They're loaded names. Queen of Heaven is one of the ancient gods the Hebrews were still worshiping around the time of Moses, likely inspiring the First Commandment: "Thou Shalt Have No Other Gods Before Me." The Queen of Fire was Zeus's sister Hestia. There was more stuff like that, but I think you'll agree with Steven that that's not interesting enough to produce a half-hour video about. It reeks of "who cares?"

But Brother Rich was determined that, if Steven wanted to expose Sherry, this was the way he would have to do it. He would need to wake the true believers from their sleep. Sherry wasn't just a false prophet. She was preaching a pagan gospel. It was an approach Steven didn't have the capacity to understand or the patience to enact. His impotence here only fed his rage, and he started to tear the whole project down.

* * *

Steven called Brother Rich a few times and left him messages asking him to respond in audio, a not-so-subtle ploy to get Brother Rich to participate in Steven's third anti-Sherry video. Even though Steven considered himself a journalist, researching and reporting weren't his strong points. For Steven, and for a chunk of the Truther community, being a journalist means collecting head-lines and videos and claiming that they're faked before revealing the "real" story that "they" don't want you to know. It's tedious, but as Steven would have pointed out, he got tens of thousands of hits on his Alternative News blog videos.

Brother Rich told Steven he should calm down, that his anger at Sherry would undermine his efforts at discrediting her and be his undoing.

"Thanks for your counsel and counseling and I respect your beliefs when it comes to the healing process," Steven told him. "I already made a prayer to The Most High, and I already made my peace with this decision on the last thing I want to do when it comes to this. I do believe that I've made it now."

Over the course of the conversation, Steven did a terrible job of arguing that his motive wasn't revenge. I think it reflects his lack of maturity. If you've ever dealt with a child who had ulterior motives, you'll get a sense of Steven's tenor.

"Right now, everybody's eyes are in our direction," he told Brother Rich. "I believe He has given us the opportunity to reveal this. You said that you have information that's going to have them running. You want to expose her, and I'd like to give you that opportunity."

Steven waited a beat.

"So, my first question is, what exactly does Sherry Shriner eat?"

Brother Rich knew Steven wasn't doing him any favors. Steven was one of the dozens or hundreds of people who denounced and attacked him. If Steven was still in the cult, he'd still believe Brother Rich was replaced. Some of the other members of the group, friends Mike had made after his expulsion, people Sherry had dismissed and attacked long ago, asked Steven to try and be happy he was out.

One woman, who emailed me and pointedly asked not to be named, wrote in a comment to Steven: "If I had come to you while you were still under her power and told you everything you're saying now, would you have believed me?" It might be the sanest thing I have heard from someone who believes in the power of orgone.

Steven couldn't argue with that logic, he didn't even try. Instead, he changed tactics, making his crusade even more noble than trying to rescue the lost. Steven said he wanted to save others from even falling in with Sherry Shriner. If people knew how she operated, Steven argued, they could avoid his fate altogether. As his rhetoric got more provocative, the group seemed to be inclined to back Brother Rich's concerns. Steven was too angry and too obsessed with hurting Sherry. He was avoiding the hard work of healing and learning from his experience, but Steven couldn't let it go.

"Isn't it more important to prevent them from even falling into this crap? Do you realize the mental torture she gives people? Dude, I had suicidal thoughts. I felt like killing myself over this," Steven said, and stumbled. That hadn't been part of the speech he'd prepared in his head. "Yeah, I'm exposing right now that happened. I felt like killing myself because of her, but I was strong enough to get through it because The Most High and His son are the main thing in my life, and I want to prevent other people from getting into that crap."

"Steve I'm just gonna say this to you, and then I'm gonna let this go. You are so eager to get even with her rather than do it the way of the Father." Brother Rich's voice was sharp with the tedium of saying no for what seemed like the thousandth time. "The Father is not about retaliation," he said.

Richard was chewing as he spoke, having lunch in his car and trying to talk a relative stranger off a ledge. He had been done with Sherry Shriner for a long time. It had cost him a lot. He took a shot at Steven's claim that he was acting on God's orders.

"That's not what He's told me. I'm gonna tell you what He told me," Brother Rich said, apparently popping the last of his lunch into his mouth. "He told me to block all this bullshit, and I'll do it."

It's a weird power struggle built around the open secret that neither of them was getting direct answers from God.

Steven didn't want to just expose Sherry and let the Lord take it from there, as Brother Rich had said. He wanted her to be as miserable and alone as he was, to know the feeling of having everyone who used to love you start hating you, to want to die the way he wanted to die, to question the point of living in a world that had nothing left for you. Plus, I don't think Steven understood much of what Brother Rich was telling him.

From Brother Rich's perspective, the only way to take down Sherry was to expose her as a false prophet. Steven didn't have the wherewithal. Instead, he undertook a campaign of name-calling.

18

DEMONS COME AND ATTACK THOSE WHO ARE ANGRY.

The thirteenth of June, 2017, was Steven Mineo's last day on the Curbside Warrior chat. He had been a member for fewer than two weeks. He'd turned thirty-two not quite a month before and had a little more than a month left to live.

His final messages to the group ache with desperation alternating with dismissal. In Steven's mind, he was spending his precious time and valuable talent trying to clear everyone's name. He would not hear anything to the contrary.

After laying out all Sherry Shriner's inconsistencies as he saw them, and testifying that Sherry made a habit out of torturing followers at random and for fun, Steven thought the only message left for the faithful to hear was that Sherry was a fat, smoking, trailer-living, shrimp-eating liar. I get where the hatred comes from, but the obsession with trying to embarrass her wasn't just transparent but also pointless.

Wouldn't it be easier, Steven reasoned, to have Brother Rich record all his religious stuff, call Sherry a fat shrimp-eater, and cut to black? Steven wanted the credit but didn't want to do the work. Legitimate research is difficult and time-consuming. It requires hours of reading background information just to get a sense of what's going on, not to mention background or at least training in vetting sources. For Truthers like Steven, the kind of digging that goes into a real-world exposé is more alien than any of the tripe they believe.

In Steven's anger and frustration, we get a picture of how many Truthers work. They find someone to say what they want. They broadcast it, headline it "Truth Bomb," and pat themselves on the back for their hard-hitting journalism.

"Let's say I was doing the interview again with Richard, while he was telling me I would learn," Steven reasoned. "So, I don't understand why I got to be put through the hard route and trying to reinvent the wheel."

Steven wanted blood, and these people kept throwing up roadblocks about anger and forgiveness.

"Demons come and attack those who are angry, just so you know," Brother Rich said. "They attack those who are angry, all right? And you could get under attack just for the simple fact that you're not understanding where we're coming from."

Brother Rich said he wouldn't do an interview until Steven demonstrated he had done the research himself and made a video. He could have said that he wouldn't do an interview until Steven sprouted helicopter blades from his head and flew away. Each was as likely.

It's unfortunate that we don't have access to everything that went down between Brother Rich and Sherry the first time. It was an experience that chastened him, I think. His wife's health weighed on him and was very likely what Brother Rich had on his mind when he told Steven to try and get his anger in check.

Maybe he didn't worry whether his own anger had called the demons to his home, but Brother Rich wasn't taking any chances. They had been under attack for two weeks, which was so much longer than Richard had intended to devote to Steven's war against Sherry Shriner. It's possible he signed on out of good cheer to gossip about Sherry and denounce her teachings, but as things devolved, he was reminded about how relentless the Shrinerites could be. I think Brother Rich just didn't want to generate more bad vibes. Spreading the truth to offset her lies was one thing but defaming her was another.

Steven, on the other hand, thought defamation was the only weapon left in their arsenal.

"I'm not listening to any more audio clips or reading anything else on here. I had something I had to say. I tried to clarify exactly what I tried to say." Steven's voice took on the tone of an exasperated mother, explaining the rules for the tenth time. "I'm more than happy to help you out, Richard, you know where to find me. You can text me or message me anytime you want on here, but I have nothing to say in this group."

Then he unsubscribed from the Curbside Warriors Facebook chat before Richard's response could post a minute later: "Obviously you've been under her power just as long as me, so you don't understand it. So when you realize that you come out from under her power and you quit doing like she's doing and do it the way the Lord wants you to do it, then we'll talk," Richard told him. "I'm out. I'm shutting you down. You ain't got to talk to me no more. I'm tired. I've got other things to worry about."

Brother Rich and the rest knew they didn't have the will to fight. That's not to say that they surrendered, only that they no longer had the vicious hearts to compete in a war of attrition. From Brother Rich's perspective, the best path was to just do their own preaching and undermine Sherry by providing real and true information. And, just in case you forgot, the real and true information was still about lizard people, giants, and monsters, just without the prophet.

* * *

The first two weeks of June had been difficult on Steven. First, his videos hadn't done the damage he had thought they would. We all have an instant aversion not just to being wrong, but to having been wrong. Think of something simple, like the immediate flash of anger having your grammar corrected by another adult. Now magnify that feeling with something more complex, like being cheated on or lied to by someone you trust. There's a bewilderment in there, but also a simmering rage. Anger at the transgressor, sure, but compounded by anger at yourself for being gullible, for trusting without reason. Most of all, for having ignored the evidence every time it bubbled up into your consciousness, little inconsistencies you let go, small lies you rationalized into the truth. We've all been there in one way or another.

The difference here is that nothing Steven believed held up, and Steven just didn't have the wherewithal to cope. I'm not even certain he had the capacity. That's why he directed all of his rage at Sherry Shriner. She was the big lie. She had manipulated him, made him complicit in his own emotional destruction by not only encouraging, but also validating his fantasies.

Imagine Steven harvesting some piece of electronic junk to refurbish, knowing that with his skill he could get enough money from it to make more orgone or, even better, to send Sherry a couple more dollars. Imagine him in his messy, claustrophobic trailer in rural Pennsylvania, looking around at what he did to himself with Sherry's encouragement. She told him the Poconos were the place to move. He hadn't dreamed of moving there before Sherry encouraged him.

Barbara was openly not a huge fan of the place. The only thing Tobyhanna had going for it, from her perspective, was that it was cheap, and Steven was there. He had made so many bad decisions based on Sherry's truth. And that was just the beginning.

Imagine almost everything you have said for the last eight years made you feel foolish. Every time you close your eyes, or your mind wanders, you remember the looks on people's faces when you talked about the power of orgone, or the NWO, or coming martial law and economic collapse. Every expression from another person you took to be ignorance was actually pity or disdain. All of your interactions have different context after a revelation like this.

These were the nagging inklings just below the surface of his consciousness, a constant "If the Easter Bunny isn't real, what about Santa?" connection trying to find purchase. Like anyone else, Steven's rage wasn't fueled as much by the betrayal as by its implications. He was at a loss and needed a win. And for better or worse, Barbara was the only ally he had left. The only person in the whole world upon whom he could count. It was a role she tried to fill by advocating all over the internet for him.

Immature as she may have been, Barbara seemed to know that the only resolution was to get Sherry Shriner out of their lives. If Steven had broken things off with her, Barbara would have moved on. If he broke it off because he believed Barbara was a lizard, I think she would have moved on all the faster. But Steven didn't.

He was committed to his fake marriage vows, more committed than Sherry was capable of imagining. Sherry's family was a burden, a reminder of her failure as a journalist, her failure to find a good provider, her failure to make anything of herself in a way that mattered to people who weren't on the fringe of accepted reality.

I don't know how many people in Barbara's life had given up as much as Steven did for her, but she recognized and returned loyalty in a way that Sherry never could. So when Steven asked a big favor, of course, she obliged.

In addition to reaching out to a YouTuber named Daniel Ott and other mid- to upper-echelon internet conspiracy thought-leaders, Steven renewed his request for Barbara to ask Sarah Adams.

Barbara poked her head into Sarah Adams's virtual office again.

"I hate to bother you. But My husband wants me to ask you for a favor," she wrote. "I told him I dont know that you would be ok doing this. He wants to post 2 youtube videos on your page. Just let me know what you think about it or would be ok with it."

Sarah consented to look at the video, and Barbara sent it along. I think if you watch enough amateur conspiracy videos, it deteriorates your aesthetic, and if you watch and make only amateur conspiracy videos, you can't tell what's watchable. I've seen a ton, but very few all the way through.

Many are auto-voiced—a computer-generated man or woman reading aloud as the words appear on the screen. Few are shorter than thirty minutes, and many span two hours or more. The images tend to be stolen, poorly sized and Photoshopped, and evocative if you're already on board with the whole scene. If you told me tomorrow that every one of them was an avant-garde art film condemning paranoia, I'd believe you. The ethereal tones, the grainy footage, and blurry pictures would be comical if they weren't also life-destroying.

Sarah hedged. She had a problem with Steven's avatar being anime, among other things.

"I'm going to chat with her and ask her to act better I am not happy with her however and she knows this," Sarah wrote. She didn't agree to post the video, though she didn't make an outright denial.

"Yes I understand." Barbara let the brush-off pass and changed the subject. "Is it true that you once resurrected a baby? [Sherry] said this."

"Yes, I have. I have others." Even in print, Sarah's voice takes on the kind of medium's other-worldliness associated with movie psychics. "There is much I can do I do not speak about."

Barbara said she would wait until Sarah had a chance to speak with Sherry, adding that the accusations and the harassment were starting to get to her a little bit and to Steven a lot.

"Lol. Don't worry about it. I honestly would just go do my thing and avoid it," Sarah said. "I have power over life and death she knows this to an extent and thus only those divine can. Evil has no such power."

Sarah disengaged from the conversation. Barbara commented twice more without acknowledgment or reply. Nearly fifty minutes later, Steven sent one of his voice messages.

"Hey, how ya doing, Sarah? This is Barbara's husband, I asked her if I could give you a transmission."

Steven runs down the story. How Sherry was attacking Barbara, and how he had discovered she'd done the same thing to others. He asks if she will post his videos to clear his name.

Sarah did not respond.

* * *

Steven was all the way out of the Shrinerite orbit now. It would have been the perfect time to walk away. Instead, Brother Rich's betrayal was thrown onto the fire with Sherry's, providing him more hate fuel and more resolve. Steven posted this:

I will "TRY" to get out a part 3 video on exposing Shriner. But i do not know when that will come out. Richard Brown has the "smoking gun" info on her and we are waiting for him to expose her completely if he ever [does]. He is holding back "extremely important info" that he says will get people "running away from her" And for whatever reason he is withholding this information. I have new info about Shriner but i am trying to learn more before i make the new video. I will try to keep this blog more up to date. Please keep a eye on this blog every few days are so. Thank you and God bless.

He posted that Sunday, June 18, almost five days after he quit the Curbside Warriors chat room. Steven was working on another approach. He knew he didn't have any real hope of getting another interview with Brother Rich, especially after how he responded to Steven's final offer of help, but he did have the audio from their conversations about Sherry.

Steven's post sent a message to Sherry, Brother Rich, and anyone else who might be listening: "I'm pressing on with this. I will not relent."

What I wonder still, though, is whether he believed Brother Rich would ever make the video Steven demanded of him, or if it was just a threat for Sherry and an invitation for people to wonder what Brother Rich had on her. Steven knew he had at least one video left in him, and he set to making the big one, the one that would take Sherry down. He didn't need Richard or anyone. He only needed time. Steven would work on his next video over the course of the next two weeks. In the meantime, there were other ways to fight Sherry Shriner.

* * *

Without Steven, the active members of the Curbside Warriors were Brother Rich and some former Shrinerites who had joined simply for support and community. They hadn't signed up for the madness that ensued. They seemed to feel bad for Steven, knowing how much more he'd endure before he realized Sherry still held sway.

The group was idle the day after Steven quit and may have stayed that way except for Steven's very public tantrum. He went on something of a spree, trolling Sherry wherever he was able, making personal attacks against her and her cult. One of them said aloud what couldn't have been more plain, something that Steven had heard but not believed.

"Honestly I have never met one person who felt better by attacking someone who wronged them ... they feel guilty later," she told the group. "Forgiveness is not just for the person who did wrong but for the one in pain. I am all for telling the truth about Sherry's lies but not about attacking her. And attacking Sherry like I saw in posts today is just cruel ... calling her a 200 lb fatass; it's not doing anything but harm."

Steven had been messaging Truther influencers from outside Sherry's circle and trying to get permission to share his videos on their pages. Against all reason, Steven thought more juice would be enough to bring down Sherry's entire ministry. It's pitiable to watch him bang his head against this doomed solution. People aren't drawn to Sherry by facts. They don't comparison shop or check reviews and ratings. In fact, the more under siege she is, the closer to the truth she must be getting.

The "fatass" crack may have referenced Steven's message to Tom Jacobs. In Steven's absence, Tom was getting more and more credibility in the group for sharing links to Sherry's shows the way Steven had. Tom often posted things like, "Sherry's Show, Uploaded Yesterday, already has 1,000 Views and Over Likes. Yyyyyeeeaaahhh!!! Sherry Shriner is The GREATEST!!! Looks like Word is Starting to get Out. MOTIVATING," and other inane cheers and flattery. After his ouster, Steven called Tom on it.

"Sherry Shriner is NOT the greatest like you always constantly say!!!" he wrote.

The amount of exclamation points and all caps that surround Sherry had to have an effect. It's a part of digital life for many that an expression be amped up to make it feel more real, more genuine. It makes sense that, to outsiders who have trouble communicating with real people in their real lives, this over-emoting worms its way into a feedback loop transforming internet reality into reality.

"You worship Sherry Shriner and she can't save your soul! Wake up man! Look at the videos!" Here Steven posted a link to one of his anti-Sherry screeds tagging Tom Jacobs. Below it, he posted another link and the jibe, "You see dude, you worship this fat 200 pound false prophet! Your salvation is at risk."

Steven sure was obsessed with Sherry's weight. It very well may come from an adage about not trusting preachers who get fat while their congregation gets thin. I think it might be something else, though. Steven didn't know any better way of hurting her, so he resorted to schoolyard name-calling. He never denounced her as a smoker or as a shrimp-eater. Obese and living in a double-wide were Steven's go-to digs.

It's at once a picture of his anger and impotence. If you could have hypnotized Steven, sat him down, and asked what he was doing, he would have told you he was exposing the truth about Sherry Shriner. The problem was he no more had the capacity to expose the truth than he did to come up with a witty insult.

Sherry had had enough. Her minions had been handling Steven. This kind of thing was supposed to be below her. Her response encapsulated everything anyone ever needs to know about conspiracy theory profiteers.

"So someone sent me a screen shot of the Richard Brown on your video," she wrote to Steven. "I've traveled all over Ohio with Rich Brown and that IS NOT him. You're so desperate to attack me you'll use fakes and liars to do so, that's pathetic, but I really don't expect anything less from you at this point."

Steven furiously told Sherry that she was the one who was desperate, that's why she kept making a big deal about Barbara's food post and was pretending that he had the wrong Richard. He was still acting as if this were about the food post—a belief he would take to his grave. It was the end of his response to Sherry, after swearing that he would keep making "truth videos on you," that his desperation became apparent.

"If you make a public apology about the LIES you are saying about my wife and the others then I will forgive you."

Is that all? He still believed there was a reconciliation possible and that he could dictate its terms. That he would accept everything else about Sherry. That he would forget that she was an evil clone or a reptilian, if she would just recant. In everything that followed, the headline-worthy narrative was that Steven wanted to die because he thought Sherry was a reptilian. He may have said she was a reptilian, but he never acted as if he believed it.

For Steven, Sherry was a person with feelings that could be hurt, who could recant and be redeemed, who could reconcile. Steven was a follower of Sherry Shriner—that's what he was best at. That's what made him worthy and important. Without Sherry, Steven was nothing and he knew it. He just didn't know how to fix it or why it happened, a snared animal who doesn't understand it's trapped, only that it's stuck and afraid.

No one thought Steven could win. I'm not even sure Steven did, but he was going to burn himself as hot as possible before he lost. He screen-capped the exchange as evidence and reposted it on his page.

"See for yourself how desperate Shriner is to hold on to her false Ministry about herself. The more views those truth videos get I made on her, the more money she is losing in donations."

Below that a commenter wrote, "Boom," and it's hard to disagree. He still could hit Sherry in the wallet, and that had to make an impression. She did, after all, have a hefty donation apparatus. If Steven prolonged this as he had been, not just on his own pages but on others' as well, it could make a dent. It's a lot easier to get people to keep giving you money than it is to get them to start.

19

I'M SURPRISED YOUR VAMPIRE WHORE HASN'T SOUL SCALPED YOU ALREADY.

Steven knew that he'd lost Brother Rich, though Sherry didn't seem to. Steven was anxious to replace him. He needed new allies and new ways to attack. More than new allies, Steven needed a stable reality, but he was inching closer and closer toward the gap between the reality he created and the one we inhabit, where questions of faith and questions of fact are sometimes irreconcilable.

For better or worse, Steven sought help from someone for whom that was never a problem.

Laurie Alexander describes herself as a "Christian eschatologist" who fights against the New World Order. Eschatology is the study of the end times and what happens to you after you die. Soteriology is the study of what it takes to be saved—in this case, how to please God enough to gain admittance to heaven.

Laurie talked a bit about both on her popular YouTube channel and Facebook page, but doomsday is her primary interest. She considers herself one of the Watchmen tasked with interpreting the signs of the coming apocalypse.

It took me a while to get in touch with Laurie, who would be an integral part of Steven's last days. In 2018, following everything that happened with Steven and Barbara, Laurie was driven underground. Her Facebook page and YouTube account fell victim to anti-Truther purges. Not long after, her in-laws were murdered. Neither a motive nor a suspect emerged, and, although she doesn't believe it was related to her online activities, it took her a while before she was comfortable giving interviews again.

Laurie doesn't have any personal photos on her pages. Her avatar is a stunning, slightly smug, comic-book blonde with a beauty-marked right cheek and full red lips. A white rabbit on her left shoulder wears a top hat and pince-nez. The words *Follow Truth and God* surround the avatar with *Follow* and *Truth* in the top corners and *God* in the bottom center. The original artwork is titled *Alice in Wonderland.*

In the zoomed-out version, a grown-up Alice wears a watch necklace and appears to be kneeling in the middle of the woods. She's surrounded by rocking-horse flies and talking flowers, and her left arm bears tattoos of the suits of cards, the heart broken in half. In the shadows an animal that looks creepy even for the Cheshire Cat fades into sight, eyes glowing a troubling blue and sharpened teeth filling its trademark grin. The art is signed, but the signature is impenetrable.

Laurie actually got a little questioning over the art from some commenters. One said it was a trigger (it's not hard to find videos explaining how *Alice in Wonderland* is laden with NWO messages), but Laurie blew the criticism off. She said she chose the image because she was always going down rabbit holes. There was no reason to change it just because the elites turned it into something bad.

The rabbit hole everyone, me included, seems so fond of going down is only fun because it's pointless. You're making up a story as you go along based on sections of previous stories that may or may not be connected. Going down the rabbit hole is weird and nonsensical, not illuminating.

Laurie believes, with Sherry, that aliens are real, but not from another planet or galaxy. They are from another dimension: hell. She resides firmly in the aliens-are-demons camp and has proof to back it up. Theological proof, not just the claim that she's spoken with God in person. Laurie doesn't claim to travel to heaven and get direct orders from the big guy himself. She falls a lot closer to the pray-and-the-Lord-will-inspire-you end of the spectrum. It's an important distinction.

Although there's an aspect of having been anointed in Laurie's claim that she's a Watchman, as far as I could tell she doesn't claim the gift of prophecy or that she's divine. Think of her title: eschatologist. Laurie is a self-educated end-times scholar.

"They're not extraterrestrial. They're interdimensional. They have crossover between dimensions," she said in an interview. "Even if you look at people who have been supposedly abducted by aliens, if they are saved, and they invoke the name of Jesus Christ, and they rebuke these spirits, they are immediately let go."

I don't want to quibble, but Sherry Shriner would agree. Prayer can protect you from being abducted by aliens. It had protected her before she discovered orgone. Sherry would argue that orgone worked better because it kept you from ever being put in a position where aliens were even in your room abducting you.

Laurie Alexander had more than 40,000 YouTube subscribers and a quarter of a million Facebook followers (pre-purge). Steven was one of them. He wanted her to share his videos and turned to her for counsel as well when he started running out of allies.

"I built myself a reputation where people knew who I was," Laurie told me. "And that's why I believe he reached out to me, because he knew that I was someone that wasn't involved with her. I can't be brainwashed by her because I had her number, basically."

Laurie doesn't identify with a denomination and doesn't consider herself an evangelical. She's a Watchman, a Bible literalist who looks for signs of the coming apocalypse "where biblical prophecy meets the headline news." False prophets are a significant last-days sign, so exposing Sherry wasn't just Laurie helping Steven. She was fulfilling her vocation.

"The Bible is clear when it says that if the Watchman fails to warn the people and somebody dies, their blood is on that Watchman's hands," Laurie said. "And I take that seriously."

Seriously enough that she joined Steven in his attacks on Sherry, hammering on her false doctrines and her obsession with orgone. Laurie didn't know that orgone was Steven's last chance, a critical string allowing him to inhabit two different realities. She only knew that he was endangering his soul by continuing to keep it around.

"I told him there was no biblical evidence that any rock will save us," she said. "I challenged him to show me where in the Bible it told us to create these rocks."

Orgone, like a cross or a statue, is a graven image banned in the Bible. Laurie said it also creates a false sense of protection. As hard as it must have been to hear, this message had to make sense to Steven. Of course, as a consummate follower, everything made sense to him. I just don't think he understood a lot of it.

Laurie had powerful friends and was tagging them and commenting on Steven's anti-Sherry posts:

[Sherry] Uses the ploys of Satan—mixing truth with lies to get true believers to follow her and support her. She is a con artist. She is not doing the work of the Most High. Her father is the father of DECEPTION, LIES, DIVISION and CONFUSION. Anyone coming on this post to defend her or to threaten Steve in any way needs to know he is protected by the Most High. No weapon formed against him shall prosper. He is covered by the Blood of Yahushua and your threats are powerless here.

Steven wanted protection more than anything else—some assurance that he wouldn't be dragged to hell for some transgression he didn't understand. If Sherry was an evil false prophet, Steven's soul was in mortal danger. It also was in danger if she was telling the truth. It may have been too much for him. Steven liked things simple. Make orgone, praise Yah, fight the NWO. That's why he wanted Brother Rich to explain how Sherry was using pagan names and rites, and that's why Laurie's claim that orgone was evil was a problem.

Over the course of the previous month, Sherry had told him he was married to a witch. Brother Rich warned him that he could be possessed when he was angry, and Laurie said orgone lets demons into a person's life. It's like finding out that your cross is radioactive, except the cancer is spiritual. Everyone knew so much more about metaphysics than Steven, and the little he did understand very well may have contributed to his death.

* * *

Although she claimed to have no designs on Steven, I think MJ, the Shrinerite from Louisiana, saw him as a good match. After all of her failed relationships, to have a man as committed to Sherry as she was had to be a dream she didn't dare give voice. After Steven's exile, MJ dipped into the fray on Steven's page when he posted the first video. She was disappointed, but willing to leave room for Steven to return to Sherry.

"Their reasoning shows clearly that they are not fully understanding the war that has just broken out among the Warriors. Yah said this would happen. They need to move on like you said," MJ said. "Steve has to journey the path that will ultimately bring him to understand what he must learn."

"Did you even watch the whole video?" Steven was incredulous, disappointed, and frustrated all at once. "You're just miserable because you can't find somebody. Give me a break. I've been a supporter of Sherry Shriner for 14 years. Don't give me your garbage."

But it was out there: "They" need to move on. "Steven" has to journey the path.

Barbara started messaging MJ at nearly 2:00 a.m. June 30. It seems she had been drinking, both because of the hour and the stream of consciousness vibe her diatribe had, doubling back on itself, referencing things that Barbara may have thought but not said, trailing off and picking up again elsewhere.

I imagine she and Steven propped up in bed, faces lit by their phones and bodies by the blue light from the TV, maybe even joking with one another about what they were seeing online or what they had said.

"I'm curious to know why do you move to the Philippines where there are no orgone warriors out there and then complain about it???? That's why Stephen Mineo is in love with Barbara Rogers who you idolize," Barbara wrote. "Hah, Hah. hah, You thought you could Kiss Sherry Shriners Ass and have had Steven Mineo hah, hah. Hah, hah Steven Mineo is mine and that's why he blocked your loser Ass. Why does he prefer a reptile over you. Because you a fucking loser. I say you stick with Cesar Masias lol."

There was more, but you get the picture. MJ woke the next morning to Barbara's rant. She was furious, she still is, but her response was measured and a little goading: "Wow. Why are you messaging me know? Mad at something? I only gave Steve a compliment ONCE a long time ago and that was it. We never even had so much as a flirty exchange. You know why?"

MJ continued typing in a pointed fury, "Because he lives over a thousand miles away, and I'm never moving from my home! All we ever had in common was that we were orgone warriors I don't care what you think of me or Sherry. Move on already. Insecure witch."

Later that morning the entire screen-captured conversation showed up on Sherry's Facebook page. Too many people pointed out that Barbara admitted being a reptile to call it a case of humor-lessness. Now there was evidence in her own words. More than a few commenters pleaded with Steven to see the light, dump Barbara, and come back into the fold, but it only spurred him forward.

"Sherry Shriner EXPOSED By Her Own Followers!!!! PART 3" debuted on Steven's YouTube page on July 1.

I suspect he re-cut some of his conversations with Brother Rich as a way of getting him to participate against his will, because this one got to her. Richard's recorded responses to Steven some-times dipped into gossip about Sherry's husband and kids, and now that Steven was out of the group, maybe he picked the most cutting ones. It must have been designed to hurt her. And I think it succeeded. Sherry was furious.

He'd stuck it to Sherry, and people were starting to notice. In their last conversation, Steven and Sherry traded threats. His weren't anything insightful, but Sherry's words would stand out when she later lamented his death and emphasized their close-ness.

"I finally got around to the list you sent me and every one of those links that you posted in that email I posted underneath all of the viral videos that are in the millions on those YouTube's pages," Steven wrote. "I posted a link to all three videos I have up on you that's exposing the false prophet that you are!!!"

Then Steven struggled to sound as if he both understood and believed the little he remembered from Brother Rich.

"When you call yourself the queen of fire the public is now starting to realize that you get that garbage from the circle of twelve of the greek gods and goddesses. You will be held account-able by the Most High one day!!!!"

Sherry's response was simple.

"Coming from someone who's lucky to still be alive, count yourself blessed. I'm surprised your vampire whore hasn't soul scalped you already. Father's anger won't hold out much longer on you. I put my enemies in His hands."

I think of this as Steven's final test of faith. He had to be torn between what he wanted to keep believing about Sherry's teachings and what he continued to learn was the truth about her, but I don't think it was simple for him. Steven's doubts haunted him as did the realization he was out of his depth.

The fight spilled over into the weekend, and there were public and private skirmishes between Steven and Sherry throughout. After his video came out, Sherry spent a second day on her Facebook page denouncing Steven:

> Should I really just start naming names [of] everyone I thought or knew who was a troll for the gov while acting like they were Orgone warriors and my best friends on the planet? Why doesn't Rich Brown expose himself for being the FBI informant that he was? For getting out of prison to infiltrate the Orgone Warriors? Or Steve Mineo, who was always so afraid I would know who or what he was … so I played their games. As I do others with these people. I wasn't born yesterday. But I also can't babysit a public list of over 3,000 people on it. And most the time you just sit back and wait for them to reveal themselves for who or what they are. When they lose relevance they'll try and keep a paycheck by becoming haters. I mean seriously folks, if you don't like someone do you make it your life's mission to hate on them? What's the real reason? $$$$

I have to say that this is the boldest statement I've seen Sherry make. It might also be the least self-aware among pages and pages of unselfconscious drivel. Sherry's MO was to find someone she didn't like and hate on them until people sent her more money. She was just much better at choosing targets than was Steven.

From Don Croft to Kelly Pingilley to Richard Brown to Steven Mineo, targeting victims appears to have been one of Sherry Shriner's favorite and most lucrative pastimes. Think of

Mike Hall's perspective: not only didn't he make a nickel trying to tear her down, he lost the few new friends he had made. Sherry's scorched-earth tactics left her victims in shambles, alone, and wishing they had never heard the name Sherry Shriner.

* * *

Steven called a private investigator in Akron, an hour or so north of Sherry's house, on July 6, 2017. When the investigator returned the call, he began the interview asking why Steven needed his services.

In the recording of the conversation the police obtained, Steven explained his predicament. The short version was that he needed video of Sherry Shriner smoking and needed Sherry to confirm her identity on that same video without knowing she was being recorded. He made an explanation about being a follower of hers and listened as the investigator explained what he would and could do, including following her to work and catching her out on a smoke break. Then he explained how hiring a private detective works.

"You would probably want, um, at least ten hours of time, in my infinite wisdom I would say twenty hours, but you can start off where you want. Our price that we charge is $85," he told Steven. "Twenty hours of time would cost you $1,700."

The number was a gut punch, and you can hear Steven take it over the line. There was no way he could justify spending $1,700 for a minute-long video of Sherry Shriner smoking. Steven negotiated for four hours of time as something he thought he could afford. Travel time back and forth from Akron to Sherry's house would have cost Steven two hours and change. The odds that the private investigator could arrive in time to video Sherry smoking and saying her name in that window feel long.

Another reason I suspect Steven never got the results of the investigation is that he called the private investigator Thursday evening, just before the end of the day. The morning of Tuesday, July 11, he posted his fourth and final anti-Sherry exposé entitled "Sherry Shriner Supporters Are Mentally Sick!" If he had the damaging video, you would have expected something like "Sherry Shriner Caught Smoking in Her Trailer!" or something like that. From the context, I wonder whether he just talked about the hate mail he was getting, hoping that naming the haters would at least make them think before sending more.

"I used to be a supporter of Sherry Shriner, and so were a couple others, but we got kicked to the curb and now we've got all these lies that are being set on us: for example, FBI and high-level witches, and all this crazy stuff," Steven wrote in a post. "Everybody that supports her has lost their minds. Look at these people's comments. You'll see it. They're no longer truthers, they are worshippers of Sherry Shriner, and they are mentally ill people."

Whatever the content, it got to her, which makes me kind of happy. Sherry put out about three shows per week. She didn't do any more while Steven Mineo was still alive. Although the video is gone, the post itself remains. Beneath it, in 24-point lime-green type, Steven wrote: "Marianne Mulloy paid for Shriners Land." Maybe he also rehashed some of the gossip Richard had shared with him, that Sherry might not be using all the money she was sent to make orgone, the extent of her reliance on funding from Marianne and Beverly, the trailer, the weight, everything. It must have been brutal to watch.

Saturday, July 12, Steven posted a new video he called "Return to Sender." It may as well have been titled "This is the First Day of the Rest of Your Life." It was a complete rebranding. There was nothing religious in it at all. Steven was back to his older self, anti-NWO warrior and how-to prepper. He and Barbara produced a video about how to undermine those bastards at the post office and assert your God-given rights to ignore tyrannical governments and junk-mailers alike.

Set to the Elvis Presley song of the same name, the video opened with Steven in voice-over, his camera trained away from him into the woods beyond. As the camera swayed, considering the pines and the underbrush, Steven said this was a "trick a lot of people may not know" and went on to explain how to return unwanted mail without having to buy a stamp.

Steven cut away to a photograph of a real-life example. It was a letter to him, marked with the seal of the Municipal Courts of New Jersey. He taped a Second Revolution insignia over his address and wrote this next to it in all caps that still managed to look like scrawl: "I rebuke your tyranical court in the name of the Most High God, Yahuah"

Steven affixed a Second Revolution-style American flag between that and RETURN TO SENDER in inch-high all caps emblazoned across the top and NO CONTRACT in letters two inches high just below it. Each word was underlined for emphasis. I wonder how many pieces of mail like this clerks of the court all around the country get? I'll bet it's more than you'd think.

The clip ends with a hand giving a thumbs-up, and this is where my story should end, too. Where Steven and Barbara go on making videos and going to the bar, find a place off the grid, and settle in to wait for martial law and total economic collapse. But that's not going to happen in this timeline. Timelines were something Steven had been returning to of late, revisiting some of his old videos about the Mandela Effect. Then, on Friday, July 14, nearly a month to the hour that he resigned from the Curbside Warriors, Steven got in his last argument with Sherry Shriner's hordes.

20

HAVE FUN DRINKING THE KOOL-AID
YOU CULT MEMBERS!

Ubaka Peter appears to have been explaining how Barbara admitted to being a reptile. Steven came across it and responded not long after he and Barbara arrived at Lombardi's, the bar down the road.

"UBAKA YOU ARE A NUT JOB!" he wrote. "Barbara is not saying she is a reptilian or a witch etc. I have video on this."

Steven had been restless and wanted to get out of the house. He and Barbara walked to Lombardi's, and the summer night was just as it should be. The cool was coming on easy as music and laughter drifted their way. They made themselves comfortable inside, ordered a couple of drinks, and conspired together.

Barbara remembered noticing Steven's attitude had improved since they left the trailer. Steven had won the headphones in the claw machine on a night like this an eternity ago, before being attacked by persons unknown and then dismissed by Sherry Shriner. His life had been taken apart and rebuilt in a mere fifty-five days.

Steven was going back through old posts, finding new fights to have. One by Marianne cut deep. She had Steven's number and wouldn't relent once she knew she'd stuck him. She talked about knowing Barbara was an agent from the start.

"But what's weird is they targeted Steve who was always a fake anyways," she said. "I don't get it."

As Barbara watched Steven engage with Ubaka and then Marianne, Steven's mood darkened. He flitted from post to post telling people (in blocks of angry capital letters) to watch the video, that Sherry was a liar and a fraud, that they all would go to hell if they didn't run away from her.

Bartender Courtney Tigue didn't notice or remember much about them that night except that they were quiet and that Barbara ordered a Bloody Mary at last call. It was a drink choice that would ring with symbolism in the weeks that followed.

But at the time, Courtney only remembered it as a complex drink for last call. She couldn't remember what Steven had, so it probably was something easy, like a beer or a rum and Coke. If she noticed him grimacing into his phone, she didn't remember.

Steven went on a multi-post tirade, calling out and mocking a couple of the members and letting them all have a little unfiltered truth, but it was just a rehash of what he'd said from the beginning.

"Sherry Shriner is an obese cigarette smoking liar!" and "It would be so funny to see your faces when you finally realize the truth about her some of you might even lose your minds."

Finally: "The heavenly father knows that these are lies being said on us that you people believe and he's giving us the honor of exposeing her!" It was nearly last call. "Have fun drinking the Kool-Aid you cult members!"

A little after 11:00 p.m., he reposted his "Mentally Sick" video, his final word on the matter, and the couple made their way out into the night.

* * *

I can picture Steven going over it all with Barbara on the walk home, shaking his head and continuing the argument under his breath. Barbara said they had a few drinks at the bar, but they must have kept drinking when they got home, because by 2:00 a.m. Steven was hammered.

Barbara had some Kratom (one of those internet drugs of dubious efficacy) she bought online. Some people smoke it, others make it into a tea or tincture. There's no agreed-upon safe dosage, but Steven was ingesting it that night in amounts that have been known to be lethal. He was high and drunk and continuing to go on about Sherry, Marianne, Ubaka, and the whole lot.

Steven was enervated as he recounted his recent trials. Drunk, despairing, and furious all at once. He started digging under the bed and pulled out his bulletproof vest and his .45 caliber Glock. Barbara had a .38, but he wanted to demonstrate a specific facet of his. Steven's Glock had a safety catch that made it impossible for the gun to go off unless someone pulled the trigger. It had a half-moon guard that ran along the edge of the trigger's arc so that unlocking and pulling the trigger were the same motion.

Steven stumbled outside, Barbara followed. It was going to be another one of those nights. Steven squeezed off three rounds and asked Barbara to fire the rest. She refused. I like to think she had a sense of it all there. Two depressed people, drunk, high, and playing with a handgun had to end badly, but Steven kept after her until she acquiesced, squeezing the trigger, enduring the pop that is always so much louder than you remember, and returning the gun to Steven.

He may still have been muttering about Sherry Shriner. You wonder whether Barbara was even listening anymore. There are so many competing explanations about what happened next, ranging from Steven slipping into a suicidal depression and begging to die, to Barbara assassinating him after turning into a lizard. I suspect the truth is somewhere between.

* * *

Steven burst into the house, Barbara behind, and here I'm lost in time. The only person who would survive the night never presented a clear timeline. I know from the court records that someone voice-activated "Eyes Without a Face" by Billy Idol on YouTube at 2:08 a.m. The song's just about five minutes long. It was Steven's phone, but it was Barbara's song. She played it when she was sad or sometimes when she was nostalgic. At 2:13 a.m., the song was over. At 2:23 a.m., Barbara called 911.

I speculated for some time that Steven had died sometime during or just after that song. I imagined a tragic breakup ending with a gunshot, and that very well might have been the case. I'm sure time stretched and compressed a lot during the last twenty minutes of Steven Mineo's life. But why did Steven go for his gun in the first place? What if it was during the song, or after? What if Barbara had told him she had enough of Sherry Shriner and Tobyhanna, Pennsylvania? That very well would have been the trigger that sent Steven scrambling for the gun and storming outside after the song, rather than before. If Barbara cut Steven loose over Sherry that night, this is the story that makes the most sense.

In addition to a blood-alcohol level of .15, Steven had the Kratom, which in excess can cause hallucinations as well as depression, delusion, and feelings of hopelessness and dread. In a world where you see demons and other evil creatures all the time, what do you hallucinate? In a world where you feel abandoned by everyone you ever cared about, how much more depressed can you get?

Barbara kept telling him she wanted to go to bed, if they could just get some sleep things would be better in the morning.

It makes you wonder how many nights ended this way, arguments or bad moods dispelled with stoned pleas of "Let's just sleep it off."

After they came stumbling back into the room, Steven and Barbara faced one another. He gave her the weapon, cupping her much smaller hands in his.

"Here, take this," he said, reminding her about the safety catch. "Press this, here."

Barbara didn't want the gun, but she didn't pull her hands away. She left them instead under his as he slid down, maybe stopping for a moment on the edge of the bed before continuing to the floor, looking up at her over his hands all the way down. There was a mirror behind the bed, throwing Barbara's reflection back at her. She looked tired, the bags under her eyes heavy with stress and exhaustion. All she had wanted to do was to go to bed, sleep it off, and figure things out in the morning. Barbara turned her head left, avoiding Steven's gaze.

I don't believe for a second that Steven Mineo wanted to die, whether he claimed to or not. Nor do I believe that Barbara Rogers entered the room that night with murder in her heart. I'm drawn to the possibility that Steven believed he was at a crossroad—a place where he could end this timeline and pick up in a better one.

I think of Kelly, of her belief that, with the right prayers and the right attitude, you could trade this reality for another. Then I think of Steven, up all night watching videos about the Mandela Effect, wondering about a reality that used to be, that still is, someplace. Certain that in the reality where the vinegar label says "Bragg's" instead of "Bragg," and orgone is a gift from Yah, and he, Barbara, and Sherry all get along.

A shot rang out.

Barbara Rogers started screaming.

* * *

Listening to her later as she prayed alone in the interrogation room, I don't believe she murdered him. It's hard to accept someone as weak and damaged as Barbara Rogers also was a cold-blooded killer and world-class actress. I've been struggling with this for a while, and there's no better way to say it: I believe Barbara pulled the trigger with no clear belief that Steven would die as a result, and that Steven may have encouraged her for the same reasons.

For context, Barbara also believed that Sarah Adams raised a baby from the dead and that weaponized chemtrails were killing us. But I'm not saying Barbara was too crazy to understand what she was doing. I'm saying that when a person lives their entire life in denial about the world around them, the world can start to fade away. In a world of monsters, resurrections, and orgone wars, a world where vaccination leads to horrible diseases and the government is constantly out to get you personally, a world that is only one of an infinite number of possibilities, maybe you can pull the trigger without consequence. As desperately as she may have wanted to, Barbara Rogers didn't live in that world.

Instead, she found herself alone in the back half of a rented trailer as the man she called her husband sat dead before her, head back on the bed as if in frustration about a blown call on TV, legs crossed, hands at his sides. Barbara called 911 and gave the details through her spasms of screams.

"He grabbed and he told me here, put this here," she said. She was barely intelligible at points, with screams and sobs coming unbidden through the words. "He grabbed me and told me, 'Here press this trigger.'"

Barbara relived the moment as she said it and broke into screams again. The 911 dispatcher asked if they were fighting, or if he had been screwing around. Misunderstanding the question,

Barbara said, "He was screwing around, he grabbed the gun. I didn't even want to carry it around."

"Where was he shot?"

Barbara choked on the answer to the point that the dispatcher first thought she said "face" and then "torso" and repeated both back.

Barbara managed a breath, almost collecting herself. "In the head," and then something that was more a long squeak of pain than an utterance, "Oh, my God, it went through his head, oh, God, please."

She remembered it then. The kick of the gun, the thunder in the tiny room, the bullet that brought skull and brain matter out of Steven's head and onto the bed behind him.

"It went through his head."

Her voice horrified and disgusted and forlorn all at once.

"This is a nightmare. Please, this isn't real."

Barbara either was by the door or still in the room. At one point she said she didn't know where the gun was and said she didn't want to go back in, but then sounded as if she was checking near Steven's body when she said, "It's right here," before losing it again.

The cruiser pulled up to the front of the house, and the officer made his way up the driveway to the back. Barbara surrendered. The officer cuffed her and stuck her in the back of the cruiser. Barbara's life was about to get a lot worse, and she would have to go it alone. The only person who would have come to her aid was lying in that godforsaken trailer with a bullet wound in the center of his forehead.

21

POLICE SAY SHOOTING MAY BE TIED TO CULT.

The interrogation room at the Pocono Mountain Regional Police Department was lit as you'd expect. Shadows encroached from the corners. It could be a small conference room in a mid-tier hotel.

Barbara sat alone, fidgeting as Detective John Bohrman came in and Mirandized her. Bohrman, a broad, fit man with a skeptical face and a short, businesslike haircut that diminishes the creeping gray, asked again whether she had washed her hands already, and in response to an earlier request to use the bathroom, told her they'd send her after they had a chance to swab her hands.

The interview is unpleasant to watch for several reasons. The first is, I wanted to like Bohrman better. Detectives are doing two things—trying to figure out what happened and trying to build a case for the prosecution. There are boxes that need checking, and during the interrogation, it often felt as if he were sublimating one to the other. He needed to have enough to be able to charge Barbara Rogers before he went home, yet there was a serious problem: no one knew what happened, and no one had enough information to proceed, but they did anyway.

As he took his seat across from Barbara, Bohrman knew that she had put a gun to Steven's head and pulled the trigger. She had admitted as much on the 911 call. She also seemed to admit that she hadn't called the police right away, telling the dispatcher that she had shot Steven "twenty minutes ago." Later on in the call

Barbara said she dialed 911 first thing. It's an inconsistency that had more to do with shock than with bad lying, I think.

From Bohrman's perspective, Barbara killed Steven either in a fight or after one, collected the cartridge, washed her hands, and called the police.

Barbara was baffled when Bohrman asked why she waited twenty minutes to call 911, and from there, things just got foggier. He got her to take him through the events over and over, looking for something that made sense with the evidence he had. He asked how drunk they got, and she said not very. How often they fought, she said never. "Never?" "Sometimes"—and so on, back and forth.

In her first telling, Barbara said they were outside shooting because Steven was upset. He'd been fighting with members of Sherry Shriner's cult. He fired three rounds and kept after her until she fired one as well, then they went inside. The trailer door opened into the bedroom.

"We went back in the house, and then he just starts talking to me. He's like, 'Oh, isn't that just wonderful,' and all of a sudden he just takes the gun, and he starts putting it in my hand," she continued with the story.

"So you were standing?"

"Yes."

No dice, Bohrman told her.

"We know he was sitting down when the gun went off," he said.

She repeated Bohrman's words as if they were in Klingon. Then she told him it was not possible. This is where things start to unravel. Bohrman knows she's lying in the way that veteran police always seem to. And Barbara was lying, about the drinking and the drugs, and something else, say, her final conversation with Steven. Whatever conversation happened between "Oh, isn't that just wonderful," and when he died, there's no question that she was lying, but in retrospect, I think it was just starting to occur to her then that they thought she killed him on purpose.

Of all the lies she was telling, she wasn't lying about him standing in front of her, which says more about her state of mind and recall than the facts of the matter. Bohrman let the point go for a while but returned to it at intervals, half revealing that she was wrong, half coaxing her into remembering. Bohrman took some time, but eventually Barbara admitted that Steven could have been sitting down when he was shot. From there she started to accept Bohrman's explanations about what the evidence showed.

When he got her to admit that she pulled the trigger on purpose, she was really just accepting his premise that these guns don't go off by accident. This is a specific reference to Steven's Glock. It's the feature that nearly every YouTube video about this gun shows, with demonstrators pressing the lever above the trigger to show how it works. It's ingenious.

"I know you keep saying an accident, but the gun doesn't go off by accident. Actually that would be if it fell on the floor and the impact of the floor made it go off. A gun doesn't go off by accident," Bohrman told her. "You have to pull the trigger. I carry a gun every single day. It doesn't go off. You have to actually pull the trigger, and you told me before you remember pulling the trigger, so you pulled the trigger."

His voice was even throughout, reasonably relentless as he dragged her to the conclusion that she put the gun to Steven's head and pulled the trigger on purpose while he sat with his back against their bed. Barbara fought him on it all the way, but he kept telling her that her story didn't match up with the physical evidence. They knew Steven was sitting down, they knew his hands weren't on the gun, they knew guns don't just "go off." Someone needed to pull the trigger. It was painful to hear, mostly because Barbara was pitiful without soliciting empathy.

Left alone a few times, Barbara talked to herself and to God. She wondered why, if she blacked out, she doesn't still feel drunk. She promised God she will take Steven to the casino whenever he wants, that he can beat her up if she wants, that she'll stop drinking, or just have one or two drinks, if He spares Steven's life. Her words rose and fell as she drifted between her internal and external monologue without knowing it, trying hard to remember what happened and even harder to will it all undone.

Back in the room, the detective continued, getting her to confirm that she knew the gun was loaded and that loaded guns are dangerous, continuing down the checklist for eliminating the argument that the shooting was accidental.

With the exception of convincing Barbara that Steven was sitting down, the hardest thing Bohrman had trouble getting her to admit was that she had pressed the gun to his forehead. It was something she couldn't conceive. Barbara assured Bohrman time and again that the gun wasn't right against his head, but if it wasn't pressed to his head, it was awfully close to it. The powder burns confirmed it. Bohrman was joined by Detective Lucas Bray, and the two of them had Barbara re-enact the killing, reminding her how she admitted she remembered that Steven was sitting down.

Having walked her through the "whats," they needed to get some "whys" out of her. Had Steven ever gotten rough or hit her? Maybe it was some sort of role-playing mishap? Barbara couldn't think of one reason she shot Steven.

"I reviewed this with the district attorney who would be handling a case like this," Bohrman told Barbara. "His thing is, we don't have a motive. We want to know why you did what you did."

* * *

When she was alone, Barbara didn't just pray for Steven's resurrection, she also wondered aloud why they hadn't brought her a lawyer yet. The reason was simple. She hadn't asked for one. Maybe she believed when they say "one will be appointed for you," the state appoints you one right then.

After five hours of an exhaustive interview wherein she was led through a description of what the police believed happened, Barbara was done. She wanted to sleep. On some level, she held out hope still that this was a dream, and the faster she woke up, the better.

Bohrman was interrogating a person who was living a playhouse life with a man who hunted pretend super soldiers. Reality wasn't Barbara's strong suit. Still, the one fact she clung to the longest was that Steven's hands were on the gun. When Bohrman convinced her that didn't happen, Barbara was adrift. Trying to jam what she could into Bohrman's narrative only muddied the waters.

It was simple for the detective: either she killed him, or he killed himself. Bohrman reasoned that since Steven already had the gun, if he wanted to kill himself, he would have just done it. That left Barbara as the murderer unless Steven wanted her to kill him. Earlier when he asked whether that's what Steven wanted, Barbara had given him a soft "No." He tried it again. They'd spoken about the cult a few times. Bohrman hit upon the line of questioning that tied the two together. Steven was upset because of the cult. He offered it up as a kind of compromise. A way Barbara could confess without culpability.

"Did you shoot him because that's what he wanted you to do?" he asked.

"No, I didn't think that the gun was going to go off, I didn't intend for it—" Barbara struggled. I don't know if she was lying or filling the hole in her memory with what she wished had happened. Either way, her voice was flat. She was unconvincing even to herself. "I actually just meant to take it, maybe just take it from him, and maybe put it away. It was what I intended to do. But some … somewhere when I grabbed it, it went off."

Bohrman wasn't buying and started to get aggressive. It would take another twenty minutes to make her crack, and then she did.

"You would never point an unloaded gun at someone's face, right? Would you agree with me?"

Barbara's "Yes, was I just, I just wanted to move it. I just wanted to put it away," wasn't more than a sigh.

"Did it hurt your hands when you fired it?" he asked. "Or did you have both hands on it?"

"I had both of my hands on it, both of them were on when I grabbed it—"

"And none of his, right?" Bohrman stepped on her line, needing her to confess to shooting a defenseless man in the head. "His hands were down by his side?"

Barbara let a frustrated sigh escape. He just wasn't getting it.

"At some point, both our hands were on the gun." She reiterated the story about it going off by accident, but Bohrman had what he needed. He charged Barbara Rogers with homicide and sent her to be processed.

* * *

"Police say shooting may be tied to cult"—the next day's *Pocono Record* headline set the tone for all the coverage that would follow. Sue Henry, host of Pennsylvania local radio station WILK's *Newsmaker Interviews*, conducted the most thorough post-Steven interview Sherry gave.

Sherry only did a couple post-killing interviews. I think she had the wherewithal to understand that she didn't need the traditional media, whom she hated, to get her word out. If people cared, they would come to her. If the mainstream media cited her, it was better than being interviewed. Sherry could say anything she wanted on her own channels.

Henry surfed Sherry's crazy, a skilled interviewer trying to corral a serial liar to get some insight, if not outright truth. I don't know whether you can say Henry succeeded, but it wasn't for lack of trying. During the interview Sherry is excited and excitable, struggling sometimes for words, and pitching herself as God's ambassador as hard as she was able.

"I was just trying to protect him, I was just trying to tell him this woman is dangerous, and he wouldn't listen," she said. "He got very highly insulted and thought I was disrespecting his wife. He's one of those New Jersey Italians."

Sherry's story was consistent, if fantastical. Steven was a longtime member of the group who introduced this new woman, whom Sherry didn't know. Once Sherry decided to look into Barbara's past herself, she dug through her Facebook accounts, claimed to have had a former police detective to look into Barbara, and built an indisputable case for her being a witch with a vampire-demon spirit.

"Why would you go to those lengths, though?" Henry asked during the radio interview. It is the only question that needed to be answered in this story, but Sherry dodged it, saying she was worried about Steven, that he was like a son to her. She used the word "kid" a lot to refer to Steven, just as whoever wrote those early death threats did. But Sherry also realized that this was the one question she couldn't answer because there is no answer to it where Sherry maintains this chaste, motherly relationship with Steven. Sherry didn't do the research into Barbara at first. She didn't do it for at least six months after becoming aware of Steven's new wife. Then she struck without warning.

Sherry shifted in the interview, returning to her lie about just being worried about Steven before pivoting to the real reason Barbara killed Steven and accused Sherry of running a cult.

"They want to make all Christians look bad and crazy, call them all cults," she said. "It's just another psy-op of theirs. I expose their psy-ops, and I'm getting my own."

She went on to say that she knew Barbara had killed at least four other people, and Henry tried to slow her down, reminding her that you can't just go on the radio and accuse people of murder. She could accuse the government of running a pedophile ring (which she did), but personal slander is something legitimate outlets prefer not to participate in.

Sherry got her airtime, though, and Henry let her get unhinged, which at that point went a long way to undermining her claim that Barbara had killed before. Then Henry asked Sherry about the reptilians and why she thought they were so prevalent.

"They can't hide it anymore," Sherry said. "With the merging of the dimensions, people are beginning to see these beings exist in people."

It's striking once you notice how often Sherry and her people use "they," and how specifically. When she talks about how "they" want to make Christians look bad, many Christians would agree, even though Sherry really means mainstream Christians. But it's not an accident. It's a dog whistle—a note played for those who worry that the people in their church might not be as committed to God, for those who know there's always more to the story.

Sherry had been going on about her attacks, the poisonings, the heart trouble, the stomach ailments, when Sue Henry tried to hold her accountable to her claims by asking the other big question: "Why would people go after Sherry Shriner?"

"When you take on Satan's kingdom, it's going to come at you full force," Sherry said. "And it has."

Now Sherry was as set as she had been after Kelly's death. This was the second time it could be proved that the New World Order targeted and killed one of Sherry's top followers. Her pre-mortem slanders against Steven and assertions that she all along had known he was a spy faded into the ether, and he became a soldier for truth cut down too soon. Sherry missed her Monday show, but knowing there was going to be a market for her first show following the murder, she was back on the air by Tuesday. I can't imagine she was really grieving.

"Boy, you know, kind of got the shoes knocked out of your feet Saturday, didn't you, huh?" Sherry was gleeful and surprised that anyone was shocked by Steven's death, which she had prophesied. "The news of Barb Rogers killing Steve Mineo."

Steven's death only mattered in the context of the grander story about Sherry. It was proof of her power and her divine right.

"The Father let me hear a conversation, and I don't know if I should relay that tonight or not, but he's very upset that she killed him. He was yelling, 'That,' and I'll be very frank, he said, 'That bitch killed me.' "

Sherry's story wanders between perspectives, as if she forgot which parts God showed her and which parts she learned from Steven, but here's the upshot:

Steven and Barbara were lying in bed watching a *Resident Evil* movie. Sherry said Barbara was friends with one of the super soldiers depicted. Sherry wasn't sure whether it was something on her phone or something on the television, but what is certain was that Barbara saw blood, and the demon began to manifest in her. Barbara Rogers started to change.

Steven was thunderstruck, paralyzed by terror, but he got his wits about him. And then he yelled, "Sherry was right about you! I should have listened!"

Sherry was telling this story as if she were sitting in the room, working the crowd even though she was in her kitchen or office, cigarette burning in the ashtray, poor internet connection crackling as she spoke.

"He got up and tried to run, but the thing that had been Barbara Rogers knocked him down and started beating him." Sherry revved the story into Hollywood mode.

Steven started crawling, struggling to pull himself to safety. That's when Barbara ran to get her gun. Steven made it to the kitchen and was trying to get to the door. He was up and running now, so Barbara shot him in the leg. Steven lay there whimpering.

"He didn't wanna die," she said, then quieter, as if to herself. "He didn't wanna die. And she said, 'Eff you,' and she put the gun to his head, and pulled the trigger."

We know this is a lie. Steven didn't have a kitchen nor was he shot twice, but try and inhabit the shock someone like, say, MJ had listening to that story and believing it. A real demon, like the one that had tried to manifest so many times in her, had manifested in Barbara and killed Steven.

I can't conceive of being that terrorized all the time. In fact, there's a part of me that won't accept that anyone at all believed this in a real, life-affecting way. Imagine asking someone at work the next day if they heard about the murder and having them reply, "Yeah, I heard that lady turned into a demon."

What baffles me more is that Sherry told it at all. That she spent a week pouring over the news reports, and in some instances, being a part of them. She knew the official story was that Steven was shot once in the head. Why change the number of shots? Why set your story in a place with a kitchen or anywhere there's room for a grown man to first crawl, then run, and still not make it out? With the exception of Steven being dead, she didn't borrow one fact from the official report.

I think the reason is simple. Sherry was pushing her followers, daring them to revolt. She wasn't any more beholden to the world of facts than she was to the Bible. Sherry created her own truth, building a reality that suited her and made her unassailable because all the terms were hers. It's a tempting contagion, but one that you can't accept just a little. You're either all in, or you're out.

Laurie Alexander was stunned. She couldn't imagine what had gone wrong in the few days since she'd last spoken with Steven. She never spoke with Barbara. Laurie did some interviews saying that the Shrinerites were a cult and recounting her experience with Sherry. She thinks she has a little insight into why Sherry would go to such lengths to accuse and persecute a relative nobody in the organization.

"I believe that Steve looked up to her as a mother," Laurie told me. "But I don't think she looked at him as a son."

Mad with jealousy, Sherry tried to get rid of Barbara and drove Steven over the edge along the way. It's the best concise explanation, even if it's not very satisfying. It's probably also the closest we're going to get to understanding why Barbara was targeted, but that's a long way from understanding why Steven is dead. It's a mystery Laurie didn't pursue long after the initial firestorm over Steven's death.

Laurie wasn't a stranger to death threats, but after her in-laws' unsolved murders, she accepted how dangerous and unpredictable people on the internet can be.

"I'm worried about those people that are out there that are watching their videos, who want to make a name for themselves. I was never worried about Sherry Shriner coming to my house," she told me. "It's the other ones, those fanatics watching [her videos] that I'm worried about."

It's a legitimate concern. Some people seem primed for holy war. Although more Americans claim Christianity as their primary faith than any other religious practice, individual Christians feel marginalized and attacked. From the fictional War on Christmas to the laughable mania for forcing prayer in schools, the violent and the persecuted will not be deterred. As with Sherry, there is no difference between disbelief and disrespect, to disrespect God's truth is to disrespect God. And there are biblical penalties already laid out for that.

* * *

Ubaka Peter was busy. He went back to all of the fights Steven had, all of the posts he made that claimed Sherry's followers were lemmings and that Sherry was a liar and wrote this (or a version of it): "Steve was Shot in the Head by his girlfriend Barbara whom Sherry Shriner warned him countless times about, RIP. Word to the Wise and the haters, Don't Come Against a Prophet of the Most High God."

There were at least five of those all posted and liked with a goblin's glee. The faithful had been rewarded. Sherry was a true prophet, protected by Yahuah. That Barbara killed Steven as Sherry predicted was irrefutable. And this wasn't retroactively explained, like Kelly's death. This was more like the orgoning of the New Orleans Super Bowl—a demonstration of Sherry's prophetic power.

Sherry steamrolled detractors after this. She opened up a Patreon account where, for a monthly fee, she promised exclusive content including an inside look at the Barbara Rogers trial.

Reporting on Barbara went quiet after September 2017, though, and Sherry struggled for content. Her health was failing, and winter was coming on. Sherry finally posted a photo of herself. Sitting in a fishing boat, holding up a comically small rainbow trout, Sherry was as big as Steven suspected. Nobody cared. Her following continued to grow, and in the quiet between Barbara's incarceration and her trial, Sherry looked to new victims and conspiracies. She continued growing her ministry with slander and vitriol.

* * *

That same September, a young woman named Kenneka Jenkins was at a party in Chicago's Crowne Plaza Hotel. Waiting for the elevator, she noticed she'd left her phone and keys back at the party. Her friends went after them, and by the time they got back, Kenneka was missing.

Security footage shows Kenneka staggering around the hotel, possibly looking for a way out. She bounced off walls, doors, and railings as she made her way through the hotel. It is disturbing to see.

Eventually, Kenneka stumbled into the kitchen and found her way to the walk-in freezer. It plays like a horror movie. She stepped just off-camera, but we can see her shadow. We don't see her enter the freezer, but we know how the story ends.

The tragedy is that from the moment Kenneka went missing, her friends called her family and the police. The police responded several times and, hearing that Kenneka was absolutely wasted, told her family to wait and see whether she showed up.

A few hours later, the police responded to another complaint at the Crowne Plaza. Kenneka's family was knocking on doors, intending to turn the hotel inside out looking for her. Eventually, the police and management were persuaded to look. Not long after, they found Kenneka's frozen corpse. The heartbreak is only exacerbated by the fact that Kenneka was Black, and the police refused to look for her.

Sherry seized upon the obvious psy-op. Using only her imagination and the viewers' credulity, Sherry found evidence of alien intervention. Sherry never got bored of implicating the family in her pretend murders. When she posted her findings on Facebook, she was clear that this was her opinion based on the facts available to her.

> [W]as killed at home by her sister Lakesha Harris (however u spell her name) and her mother Tereasa while James Coleman took the video. An ambulance arrived to take the unconscious or dead, Kenneka to the hospital so her organs could be harvested. Selena Gomez gets a kidney that very same week in Chicago. (Tereasa had talked to Selena 4 months earlier) This was a preplanned 'sacrifice' for Teresa, so it was recorded on K's phone which is why they would never release her phone. The Elites wanted proof of the death so the death was recorded. Teresa will now get her 'fame and fortune' for the accepted sacrifice by the Elites.

This post was my introduction to Sherry Shriner, one of the first things I saw once I started researching. It provided the lens through which the rest of the story unfolded and informed me, more than almost everything else, about her recruiting techniques. The first comment video I saw was a young Black woman, "Andria," making the case that Sherry was right, and that there was more to the story than the authorities let on. More than that, maybe Sherry possessed second sight.

"I don't want anybody to think I endorse everything that, you know, she's taught," the woman told the screen in direct address. She explained how Sherry predicted Steven Mineo's death and gave the details as proof that Sherry had supernatural influence and understanding.

"I'm just thinking, Wow! If she was right about this, shouldn't we keep an open mind and at least hear her out and watch her videos to see if maybe there was something else that she was right about?" Andria posted.

Lather, rinse, repeat. Sherry just sat back and let her new believers be her evangelists. Steven's death had given her more power than Kelly's suicide or Rich's fake death or even the Super Bowl. Steven never could have spread her word as well alive as dead, though it was all the same to Sherry. She would ride the Kenneka Jenkins conspiracy into the new year. Once Barbara's trial started in the spring, there was no telling how much attention she would get.

* * *

Barbara and her legal team decided not to take the original plea offer, which was murder in the third degree, acting with depraved indifference to human life. Pennsylvania is one of only three states with this buffer between second-degree murder and manslaughter. It's also called "depraved heart," which feels a little closer.

Depraved heart murder is acting in such a way that you know there is a genuine threat to human life. Pointing a gun at someone's head surely qualifies, but Barbara had a better than average chance of beating it. Her lawyers seized on the police investigation and interrogation, and constructed a narrative wherein the police solved the case before they went to the crime scene and contorted Barbara's statements to fit.

The night Steven died, detectives Bray and Bohrman met at the nearby Exxon to listen to the 911 call Barbara made and formed a plan. Bohrman would take the witness, and Bray would take the scene. It isn't unusual for detectives to confer on the way to the crime scene. Neither is it unusual for the police interrogator to assume everything a suspect says is a lie. The fact that they had jumped to the wrong conclusions, though, and imposed those incongruous narratives on Barbara made it a lot easier for the defense to undermine them.

Barbara comes off as pitiable in the interrogation videos. You feel sorry for her and her confusion, her stupidity. Watching the police direct her reenactment, and listening to her whispered prayers and self-talk, we see a woman to whom life has always happened. Forces act upon Barbara, and her decisions and actions are at best attempts to please and conform in advance. She guesses at what the police want, or what she thinks they want. Once she breaks, even though there is no doubt she had just participated in a death, it feels wrong, as if she were tricked.

The prosecution put on a short, straightforward case. Barbara said she shot Steven on purpose, admitted it on tape. She and Steven were cult members. Steven didn't want to die. In place of providing a salient motive, they argued that she was annoyed, and the couple was fighting. Throughout the trial, the defense used every opportunity to undermine the investigative and interrogative tactics. Once the defense called Glock expert Manny Kaplesohn, the prosecution's case began to unravel.

Bohrman told Barbara Steven's hands couldn't have been on the gun at the time of the shooting. As it turned out, Steven's hands were for a fact on the gun when it went off. That's why the police didn't find the cartridge until after Barbara confessed to shooting Steven while his hands were at his sides. It was still in the chamber, blocked from being ejected by the pair of hands that was wrapped around the barrel at the time.

Kaplesohn explained about the particular safety on the Glock. More important, he demonstrated that the only way this gun would fail to eject the cartridge would be if someone had their hands around the barrel. Juxtaposed with the detective's aggressive attempts, this revelation called everything Barbara admitted into question.

Although the crime scene officers bagged Steven's hands in anticipation of giving him a gunshot residue test, the police decided to forego it, reasoning that gun residue would have been all over that small room. It was another fact the defense disputed, pointing out that the police did one on Barbara and that the FBI still did them as well.

It may have just been an expense the investigators didn't feel they needed, just like the blood-alcohol test they didn't do on Barbara. They knew what happened. It was one of the reasons that they didn't consult Kaplesohn, who often testified for the prosecution in that very courtroom. Pointing out that he was working for the defense, Barbara's lawyers claimed the prosecution decided not to use him because he weakened their case.

While both sides acknowledged Sherry Shriner, she didn't factor heavily. As much, I think, because she didn't fit either the defense or prosecution narrative, as because this was already a court case that didn't need another ounce of bonkers.

The defense, however, used Sherry to introduce doubt about whether or not Steven wanted to die. The prosecution discounted her influence. She was in Ohio and didn't have the reach. Sherry Shriner was a specter, not a motive. This was a domestic incident where one partner killed the other. It was too common to worry about the "whys" and "wherefores." Sherry's involvement is just conjecture.

It's possible that either side would have called her. Indeed, the prosecutors were all set to meet her. We would have the pleasure of listening as Sherry, under oath, proclaimed herself the Daughter of The Most High Yahuah. But by the time Barbara's trial started, Sherry Shriner was three months in the grave.

* * *

Sherry Shriner dropped dead on January 7, 2018. She had celebrated her fifty-second birthday on December 11. The "official" word was that it was a heart attack. No one was as disappointed as I to confirm it.

From the first, I'd hoped against hope that it was not true. I'd done enough time in conspiracy theory circles to put together a solid case for her death being a hoax. True, she remained active until right around the time investigators from the Monroe County prosecutor's office was hoping to interview her, but before I even knew that, the opportunity of the New Year provided a perfect exit point.

Very few people had seen Sherry; only a couple more had even spoken with her. She could vanish from the internet and continue her ministry in a more private, insular way. Sherry had laid down such a convoluted Messianic hodgepodge that she could show back up whenever she felt like it and only have greater popularity.

Beside the death announcement on her Facebook page, there was her father's obituary from November 2018. It listed his survivors, including Arch and Sherry's kids, before saying he was predeceased by his daughter, Sherry. This didn't settle it for me in the way it should have. After all, it wasn't a death certificate (I hadn't been able to discover Sherry's), and the funeral home writes whatever you ask of them for the obit. They don't fact-check.

That was my first glimpse. I so wanted Sherry to be alive and confrontable that I imagined her entire family would consent to lying about her death in her father's obituary. Even now it feels reasonable to me. It's this sense of desire-driven reasonableness that I try and think about as I watch people sink into conspiracy thinking.

243

The story the Shrinerites tell about Sherry's death isn't less romantic than mine by any means. God told Sherry to go to her room and ready herself for bed. The prophet followed her routine, turning on praise music to enjoy as she changed her clothes. And then God just took her.

Although I've read it elsewhere, MJ gave me a detailed description, qualifying Sherry's "death." Sherry didn't die in the regular sense. She couldn't have, because that would have meant Lucifer succeeded in killing her. Instead, knowing that the devil was preparing an attack on her, God took her instead, like a bully snatching an offered sweet away at the last moment.

This version was important to them, that Sherry was neither killed by or because of Lucifer, but there aren't any satisfactory descriptions that parse the difference. In them, there's this desperation to avoid the fact that Sherry either was dead because God couldn't protect her, or because Lucifer won.

Ignoring that fact with all their might at the peril of their lives, Sherry Shriner's followers await her return with her brother and father any day now, when the world comes blessedly to an end.

APOCALYPSE

In the fall of 2020, something woke the cause, and one of Sherry Shriner's websites (BibleCodesRevealed.com) got a facelift and a new post. In addition to my own research, two documentary teams were investigating her story. It makes sense that the Shrinerites would use the opportunity to spread the word. Thanks to the renewed attention and her followers' zeal, Sherry can now preach from beyond the grave until she returns in glory with Jesus for the War of Armageddon.

The few posts have picked out news events that match up with Sherry's prophecy. Her highly searchable radio programs provide easy access to key-worded doomsdays. Sherry predicted COVID-19, a single-term Trump presidency, and, as always, the end of the world, martial law, and economic collapse. They even appear to be keeping up the work of self-division, persecuting and casting one another out over accusations and trivialities. In fact, Shelly Long might be the most recent ejectee.

A virulent Shrinerite while Sherry was alive, Shelly told Steven Mineo that Barbara being a witch was no reason to go against Sherry. In 2019, her support for Trump left her on the wrong side of the narrative that Trump was a placeholder while the New World Order regrouped. When she continued to support Trump, Shelly came under attack, but Shelly could hit back. Plus, without Sherry around, she could rebel without consequence.

She said, "[Y]our cult like bashing of those who don't take what you say as 100% gospel is what ended up in the Kelly Pingilley and Steve incident. Stop acting like cult members instead of servants of the most high. You people are treading dangerous waters."

While the website has developed, Sherry's Facebook page has gone dark for the most part. Facebook posts I've cited in my research are missing. I've confirmed with others that this isn't me being out of my mind—plus I have copies. New posts are relegated to tags from fringe followers and the occasional request for a new show. It makes sense. People don't search for Sherry on Facebook, so best to direct them to income-generating pages.

A jury found Barbara Hellen Rogers guilty of third-degree murder and sentenced her to fifteen to forty years in prison. Barbara remains incarcerated. She's still working to come to terms with her part in Steven's death. I don't know if she consciously remembers what happened, but I heard she's trying, which is better than waiting to wake up from what she hoped was a nightmare. Maybe she still holds out hope the Mandela Effect is real, and there is an alternate timeline where the gun went click but didn't fire, and Steven was no longer obsessed with Sherry Shriner, and no longer afraid of demons or the NWO.

While he's certainly beyond fear and pain, I don't think Steven Mineo still haunts the junk shops in alternate-reality Tobyhanna, Pennsylvania. Steven is dead, and maybe it always had to end that way. Maybe there's an alternate reality where he doesn't meet Barbara, but there's no world where Steven doesn't meet somebody, and no world where Sherry Shriner doesn't have a huge problem with it. From the first moment he tuned into her BlogTalkRadio show, Steven's life was on a collision course with Sherry's whims. His break with her was destined to be violent.

"Steven was on the run from a reptile cult and believed the only way he could be freed was in death" is just as informative as "Steven was murdered by a demon." "Kelly was a crazy girl, so she killed herself" is just as neat as "Kelly was murdered by her family," and almost as revealing. These are stories that could offer insight to where we are as a culture, and dismissing them as stories about crazy people is unwise.

No one who was touched by these deaths doesn't wish they had taken the signals more seriously. I'm writing this in early 2021, wondering why we thought it was funny when people said chemtrails were killing us all, but less funny when people said wearing masks against a lethal pandemic-causing virus was an NWO ploy, then stormed the US Capitol building.

Whether or not he begged to die that night, Steven Mineo had considered killing himself rather than face the truth about Sherry Shriner. He spent the last two months of his thirty-two years on this planet trying to deny that she was and always had been a liar and a fraud. But let's not judge that too harshly.

Flat earthers, Truthers, conspiracy nuts, and anti-vaxxers are a funhouse reflection of the idea that all opinions are valuable. They only can be excused as crazy for so long. The truth will out, and in this case, the truth is that we're all struggling so hard to point out awful people and actions, it's easy to forget our complicity.

Culture doesn't happen to us; we build it as we go along. We've weaponized facts, using them as bludgeons instead of as plot devices. We've cultivated a disdain for admitting error and fetishized the snappy comeback. Winning the argument is prized over understanding the dispute. Religion has failed us, and civic duty has been revealed as the greatest myth in the Western world. Truther paranoia isn't misplaced, only overwrought.

I'm not ringing the doomsday bell or claiming that modernity is ruining everything. I'm just trying to share what I learned in the Shrinerites' reality. Everyone thinks they have a good reason for doing what they do or believing what they believe. Before we make the easy joke, reveal a person to be an absolute moron, or call them out for their hypocrisy, it's wise to remember that we're building reality together, and without full participation, it's a dicey proposition.

NOTES AND REFERENCES

Much of the information used to produce this book was received via court records and other evidence gained through Freedom of Information Act requests to Monroe County, Pennsylvania, and Jackson County, Michigan. Both Barbara's and Steven's Facebook accounts for 2017 were in a digital file. There, I found photos and posts, some of which are reproduced in the photo pages of this book. I read the interactions in Sherry Shriner's Facebook chat rooms and listened to the messages Steven, Barbara, Richard Brown, and Mike Hall sent back and forth to one another.

I also used audio from Sherry's BlogTalkRadio show as well as from her public Facebook page. I viewed Kelly Pingilley's blog and archives.

In personal interviews, Rebeckah Lasak, Marcy Walsh, Britt Simpson, Brandon Moore, Nate Pingilley, Geoff Baker, Pearl Snapp, "MJ," and Shane Pettman shared with me their memories of the inner workings and power structure of Sherry Shriner's cult; and of Barbara Rogers, Steven Mineo, and Kelly Pingilley.

I made seven reporting trips to Tobyhanna, Pennsylvania, reading the transcripts in the Monroe County Courthouse and driving around, hoping that visiting the scenic mountain town's streets and hangouts would help me understand better the last, fatal spiral of Steve and Barbara. But insight remains elusive.

References

Andria's Analysis, "Was Sherry Shriner Right about Kenneka Jenkins too???," YouTube Video, 5:13, January 22, 2018, *https:// youtu.be/oHDcZnFH0OU*

Brown, Richard. This Is The Full Fledged Show. By Johnny Galvan. April 29, 2015. *http://www.blogtalkradio.com/thisisthe-fullfledgeshow/2015/04/30/interview-with-orgone-warrior-rich-ard-brown-in-ohio?fbclid=IwAR2fRD2WRFy4y6k_rUs6F-m3U04UE-IFiaCUbRBOAaJrANShNGMXv0Lva4e0*

Court of Common Pleas of Monroe County. State of Pennsylvania V. Barbara Hellen Rogers. Docket Number: CP-45-CR-0002045-2017

Croft, Don. "Sherry Shriner pitched Christians to Don Croft." *Curezone.org*, circa 2007 *https://www.curezone.org/forums/fm.as-p?i=907607***i*

CT Busters, "Don & Carol Croft with David Wolfe - Zappers!," YouTube Video, 9:49, November 24, 2009, *https://youtu.be/J_tDkallLMI*

Garry Coberly Obituary, Published by Gattozzi and Son Funeral Home, November 2018 *https://www.dignitymemorial.com/obitu-aries/chesterland-oh/gary-coberly-8055480*

Jackson County Office of the Sheriff, Jackson County, Mi. *Incident Report, Kelly Pingilley Suicide* Case number 2012-00035405. Jackson County: 2012

Keilman, John. "Lawyer claims Kenneka Jenkins might have been locked inside hotel freezer, but police video contradicts theory." *Chicago Tribune*, Dec. 19. 2018 *https://www.chicagotribune.com/news/breaking/ct-met-kenneka-jenkins-locked-inside-freezer-20181218-story.html*

Kelly Marie Pingilley Obituary Published by Charles Step Funeral Home, Jan. 2013 *https://www.charlesstepfuneralhome. com/obituary/1890473*

Kenneka Jenkins video Police surveillance released to CBS *https://www.youtube.com/watch?v=MmVYbeNyYEo&*

Kurutz, Steven. "Michael Drosnin, Who Found Clues in the Bible, Is Dead at 74." *New York Times,* June 19, 2020 *https://www. nytimes.com/2020/06/19/books/michael-drosnin-dead.html*

Lamoureux, Mark. "How Cults Use YouTube for Recruitment" *Vice.com*, Aug. 11, 2017 *https://www.vice.com/en/article/wjj85y/ how-cult-leaders-use-youtube-to-recruit-new-members*

McClurg, Lesley. "The Kratom Debate: Helpful Herb Or Dangerous Drug?" *Morning Edition*, Jan. 13 2020 *https://www.npr.org/ sections/health-shots/2020/01/13/789145948/the-kratom-debate-helpful-herb-or-dangerous-drug*

Monroe County Office of the District Attorney. *Rogers Evidence.* Eric J. Kerchner. Monroe County, Pennsylvania: Monroe County Office of the District Attorney, 2019.

Sherry Shriner BlogTalkRadiocom, multiple episodes. *https:// www.blogtalkradio.com/sherrytalkradio*

Shriner, Sherry. Truth Train with Liberty Lisa. By Lisa Brumfiel. July 12, 2016. *http://www.blogtalkradio.com/truthemerges?f-bclid=IwAR01gK4cjYeledy4rgOaNEQV3j005ie3BeRdySzrp_a_ LhKZIq_v5TLr5wc*

Shriner, Sherry. Newsmaker Interviews. By Sue Henry. July 19, 2017. *https://wilknews.radio.com/articles/sherry-shriner-wilks-sue-henry*

Pingilley, Kelly M. "FirstFruits Elect." LiveJournal.com, *https:// warrior-elect.livejournal.com*

Weill, Kelly. "Reptile Cult Leader Says Her Follower Was Killed By NATO," *The Daily Beast*, July 2017 *https://www.thedailybeast.com/reptile-cult-leader-says-her-follower-was-killed-by-nato*

Wilcox, Roger M. "A Skeptical Scrutiny of the Works and Theories of Wilhelm Reich As related to The FDA Injunction against Reich." September 2003 *http://www.rogermwilcox.com/Reich/fda.html*

Winter, Tom; Losnar, Michael and Wong, Wilson. "Feds probing whether Nashville bomber believed in lizard people conspiracy." *NBC News* Dec. 30, 2020. *https://www.nbcnews.com/news/us-news/girlfriend-nashville-bomber-warned-police-he-was-building-explosives-2019-n1252536*

ACKNOWLEDGMENTS

Kelly's friends Marcy Walsh, Brittany Simpson, Rebekah Lasak, and Brandon Walsh weren't just instrumental in helping me get my head around what happened to Kelly, their openness with me about Kelly's light and dark sides helped me to care about her in a way that police reports never could. Similarly, MJ's participation was critical, and I wanted to acknowledge her honesty and cooperation.

Radio Host Geoff Brady was generous with his time and insight as he helped me understand Sherry, Don Croft, and orgone.

As excited as I am for you to read this book, I'm all the more excited for my friends, Stephanie Fowler and Jeff Smith, to read it. They provided me with invaluable help and direction with the bulky, dense, confusing early manuscript on an unreasonable deadline. This isn't the book they read, and it is now better for their insight, support, and patience.

Katie Russo, my sister-in-law, read and commented on each draft and her insight improved it each time.

While I had so much help in making this a story that people could follow, my editor, Sandra Wendel, made it a story people would want to follow. Her infectious excitement about this book was the fuel I needed as I approached the finish line.

Ron Sauder of Secant Publishing swooped in at the last minute with solutions to problems I didn't even consider before they came up.

I was fortunate enough to cross paths with Lana Gorlitz, who was researching Sherry Shriner for VICE's documentary *The Devil You Know*, Season 2. Working on something like this, it was reassuring to be able to talk with someone who was conversant in Shrinerite. Similarly, thanks to the rest of the VICE newsmagazine production team, especially Sarah Sharkey Pearce, who gave me the opportunity to participate in the documentary, and director Zebediah Smith, who was patient and encouraging and used my own interview tricks against me right to my face. Their interest in my take on Sherry Shriner, as well as their generosity with information and sources, helped me refine my thinking about our responsibility when it comes to social media cults.

I came to the genre thanks to *Sword and Scale* host and producer Mike Boudet. When I was making the podcast *This Is War*, he encouraged my narrative sense. More important, though, he valued it in a way few publishers have. In addition to putting me onto the Sherry Shriner story, Mike helped me understand true crime is always personal and that telling the story is more important than hitting the tropes.

Professor Joerg Tuske at Salisbury University helped me understand—or at least accept—the tenacity with which some people cling to conspiracy theories. Specific to this story, he helped me think of paranoia like functional alcoholism—something that can stay hidden indefinitely.

How to tell this story was the primary question in my life for the better part of eighteen months. My daughters, Amanda Mohammed Mirzaei, Melissa Messick, Megan Russo, and Allison Russo, spoke with me about reptile people long after it stopped being interesting to them.

This book was written during a challenging year. My wife, Kelly, to whom this book is dedicated, endured my prolonged sequestrations, trips to Tobyhanna in Pennsylvania, and general angst while teaching eighth-graders in person and online during this spectacularly bizarre experience. She gave me courage and confidence every day. More than anyone else, without her, this book doesn't happen.

If you stayed on this far, thank you so much for taking this bizarre, sometimes convoluted trip with me.

ABOUT THE AUTHOR

From the first time he created a biographical sketch from source material, Tony Russo was interested in telling stories about people's everyday lives. As a journalist, he specializes in profiles and feature stories that connect people with their community and culture.

Tony began producing independent podcasts in 2007 in addition to his work as a reporter. He produced podcasts on beer, local news, and writing, always with a focus on the individual's relationship to their place and time.

In 2017, he earned the honor of writing and hosting *This Is War*, a narrative podcast about the combat veteran experience. In more than fifty interviews with American veterans of the wars in Iraq and Afghanistan over the course of the next two years, Tony wrote biographical narratives tracing the careers of men and women who had their lives changed in service to their country. Each story was astounding all on its own, providing snapshots of our country and culture at multiple times and places over the decade-plus conflict.

Tony coveted the chance to tell a story like this, that brings together questions about history, religion, politics, and popular culture, and investigates how they played out in these real-life circumstances when two realities collide. Sherry Shriner, her cult, and the insidious and violent nature of the conspiracy theory culture showed him that while truth may have inherent value, as a commodity it's pretty much worthless.

In his research, he crossed paths with a documentary team from VICE that also was investigating Sherry Shriner. In 2021, he was featured in their series *The Devil You Know, Season 2.*

Tony lives on Maryland's Eastern Shore with his wife and the only one of his four daughters who hasn't moved out. Together they keep their dog and cats comfortable.

CPSIA information can be obtained
at www.ICGtesting.com
Printed in the USA
JSHW030913280223
38294JS00001B/3

9 781944 962944